Malory's (

The story of the Grail, rich in mystery and symbolism, held the medieval world enthralled. The quest for the ineffable object reappeared often in the literature of the times, exciting the interest while embodying the changing values of its various adapters. In this analysis of one such adaptation, Sandra Ihle considers Malory's *Tale of the Sankgreal*, looking both to its thirteenth-century French source and to its author's own structural and thematic adaptation. The result is a fascinating study, one which medievalists, art historians, and students of French and English romance and rhetoric will value for its insight into medieval literary theory and esthetics, and for its novel perspective on the significance and underlying intentions of Malory's distinctive Grail quest.

Sandra Ihle is Lecturer in Professional Communications at the University of Wisconsin-Madison. A medievalist, she has presented a number of papers on Arthurian romance and medieval rhetoric.

MALORY'S GRAIL QUEST

Invention and Adaptation in Medieval Prose Romance

SANDRA NESS IHLE

The University of Wisconsin Press

Published 1983

The University of Wisconsin Press
114 North Murray Street
Madison, Wisconsin 53715

The University of Wisconsin Press, Ltd.
1 Gower Street
London WC1E 6HA, England

First printing

Printed in the United States of America

For LC CIP information see the colophon

ISBN 0–299–09240–2

Photographs by James Austin

TO THE MEMORY OF

Eugène Vinaver

Contents

Illustrations

Acknowledgments

This study did not, of course, spring full-grown from my head; it owes its impetus and much of what it contains to the encouragement and work of others. Besides determining the direction in which my work would go, the late Professor Eugène Vinaver gave unstinting help and provided an unparalleled scholarly example. His faith in me is hardly recompensed by the dedication of this book to his memory.

I would like to acknowledge as well those whose work influenced my direction but do not appear in these pages. Over a decade ago Professor V. A. Kolve, in a Stanford lecture on Chaucer, first made me aware of the structural similarities of medieval literature and Gothic cathedrals. Professor Robert Jordan in *Chaucer and the Shape of Creation*, besides carrying further the comparison between medieval literature and architecture, allowed us all to see medieval art as "inorganic," thus opening the door to investigations into the nature of its construction.

Professors Donald Rowe and Andrew Weiner of the University of Wisconsin at Madison have both read this book in an earlier version, and I gratefully acknowledge and have incorporated many of their suggestions. I have also benefitted from and greatly appreciate the helpful comments of my readers, Professor Karl D. Uitti of Princeton University and Professor Norris J. Lacy of the University of Kansas at Lawrence. Ms. Christine Sundt, slide collection curator for the Art History Department of the University of Wisconsin-Madison, assisted me in locating and selecting photographs to illustrate the text; I appreciate her gracious efforts. Finally, to my sister, Marilyn Kopperud, my great thanks for many retypings. And to Douglas, for whom I wrote this . . .

Malory's Grail Quest

CHAPTER I

Principles of Adaptation: Medieval Architecture and Poetics

Professor Vinaver has written that "Malory's *Tale of the Sankgreall* is the least original of his works. . . . it is to all intents and purposes a translation of the French *Queste del Saint Graal*, the fourth branch of the thirteenth-century Arthurian Prose Cycle."[1] And William Ryding comments on what he considers Malory's failure to change the *Queste*: "he left it structurally the same as he found it, contenting himself with a brutal reduction of the symbolic and allegorical commentary that made the Old French text more a didactic than a narrative work."[2] It is true that Malory's departures from his source in the *Sankgreal* are not so radical or dramatic as is the case in *The Book of Sir Launcelot and Queen Guinevere* or in *The Tale of the Death of King Arthur*; in these works, Malory skillfully picks out widely separated threads of the interlaced stories from his sources, making compact episodes out of narrative lines formerly interwoven with others. Nonetheless, in spite of Malory's cautious departures from his source in the *Sankgreal*—or perhaps because of them—this work serves as an excellent example of the principles of structural adaptation by which he worked. For although Malory closely followed his source for the content of his narrative and kept the original sequence of episodes, he nevertheless produced a quite different work. Its entire "shape" has been altered, and consequently the meaning also has undergone a radical transformation. This study will focus on the *Sankgreal* and the *Queste* in an attempt to delineate the compositional principles underlying each.

Thus far there have been few structural studies of either Malory's *Sankgreal* or the French *Queste*, and fewer comparisons of the two, in order to discover the techniques of adaptation Malory used.[3] It would seem obvious that any complete discussion of his art should depend upon a knowledge of the sources from which he worked. Malory, like any other medieval author, was not concerned with inventing new stories except insofar as the term "invention" may be applied to his new disposition or interpretation of the elements found in old stories. Failure to consider Malory's sources may even lead to critical distortions. For example, Stephen Knight, who states his intention "to avoid using evidence derived from source-studying,"[4] concludes that Malory is ironically juxtaposing Galahad and Lancelot at the beginning of the *Sankgreal* by placing them in close physical proximity.[5] All of the instances Knight cites, however, are already present in the *Queste*. Of course, it is true that what Malory retains from his source is just as significant for his art as what he adds or changes; at the same time, however, to analyze borrowed material as though Malory had—in the modern sense of the word—"invented" it is to ignore a primary feature of medieval writing, that of adaptation. A close comparison of Malory with his source reveals what he chose to retain, what he left out and added, and, most important, the principle guiding these choices.[6] And the discovery of Malory's manner of adaptation can point to the significance both of his work and of the *Queste*.

This study will first attempt to discover what medieval terms we can use to describe the structural uniqueness of the *Queste*. Jean Frappier, in his study of the *Mort Artu*, hypothesizes an "architect" who planned the Vulgate Cycle.[7] Although Frappier is dealing with the problem of authorship, his terminology is suggestive; in attempting to define the "shape" of a work, one is really asking how it was "built," and medieval architecture reveals how medieval artists built. Much has been written about the analogies among the various spheres of artistic endeavor in the Middle Ages, and it is quite likely that "habits of mind" influencing artistic production in one area would also mark those in another.[8] Thus, an identification of architectural principles applicable to narrative structure can help us to discover and understand the compositional principles used by the author of the *Queste*.

That the analogy between architecture and literature was commonplace in the Middle Ages is evident in Geoffrey of Vinsauf's use of it to introduce his *Poetria Nova*. There he likens the poet's need to determine the parts and order of his work prior to writing to the builder's need to follow a careful plan.[9] Since the *Poetria Nova* and the other arts of writing conceived of literary composition as "building," they provide a framework to translate architectural principles into medieval literary terminology.[10] A description of Gothic architecture contemporaneous with the *Queste* and instructions for literary composition in the arts of poetry together help define the structure of the *Queste* and Malory's adaptation of it.

A structural study will, of course, reveal Malory's thematic concerns and ideas. These have been previously studied, particularly by more recent scholars. My purpose, however, is not to credit Malory with thematic interests hitherto undiscovered but to illustrate the validity and usefulness of a method that allows us to see his adaptation as consistent with certain principles of composition. It is through an understanding of Malory's structural principles that the ideas guiding his adaptation most clearly emerge and may be found as intelligent and cohesive as they are different from those of the *Queste*. Through the use of architectural terminology and medieval literary theory, both the *Queste* and Malory's adaptation of it emerge as unique responses to the same subject: the quest for the Holy Grail.

Geoffrey of Vinsauf expresses the analogy between architectural and literary production in the general remarks on poetry at the beginning of his *Poetria Nova:*

> If a man has a house to build, his impetuous hand does not rush into action. The measuring line of his mind first lays out the work, and he mentally outlines the successive steps in a definite order. The mind's hand shapes the entire house before the body's hand builds it. Its mode of being is archtypal before it is actual. Poetic art may see in this analogy the law to be given to poets: let the poet's hand not be swift to take up the pen, nor his tongue be impatient to speak; trust neither hand nor tongue to the guidance of fortune. To ensure greater success for the work, let the discriminating mind, as a prelude to action, defer the operation of hand and tongue, and ponder long on the subject matter. Let the mind's interior compass first circle the whole extent of the material. Let a definite order chart in advance at what point the pen will take up its course, or where it will fix its Cadiz. As a prudent workman, construct the whole fabric within the mind's citadel; let it exist in the mind before it is on the lips. (*PN*, pp. 16–17)[11]

Geoffrey's concern is with the care and planning necessary for the construction of a work of art, and he goes on to describe the rhetorical means whereby a satisfactory literary work is achieved.

Underlying the architectural analogy is an aesthetic theory resulting from eleventh and twelfth-century Neo-Platonism, developed at the school of Chartres, a belief that theology could be translated into material. Platonic notions of light, number, and proportion could be used not only to represent God's truth but also to reproduce it through mundane matter. As Otto von Simson states of Notre Dame at Chartres, "We may well define it as a 'model' of the cosmos as the Middle Ages perceived it. But this 'model' was ontologically transparent. It reflected an ultimate reality."[12] A primary feature of this aesthetic is its emphasis on order and thus the palpable delineation of the parts by which a work of art is composed, and the means by which these parts are brought into harmony, a harmony analogous to that of the cosmos. Rhetoric provided these means for literary productions, and the arts of poetry articulated for authors the specific devices necessary for various kinds of order and harmony. Geoffrey of Vinsauf's participation in this aesthetic view derives from his own association with the school of Chartres and links him with the artistic ideas prevalent during the thirteenth century. Gothic architecture and medieval poetics therefore grew out of and expressed a common conception of order.

Gothic cathedrals, the most representative architecture of Geoffrey's time, bear a similarity in shape to the *Queste*. The structural elements of these cathedrals have been studied extensively by Paul Frankl, who has proposed a terminology by which to describe them. With this terminology as a starting point, we may extend Geoffrey's analogy to discover specific literary principles corresponding to the structural principles of Gothic architecture. The rhetorical tradition was the source of the art of composition for medieval romancers; therefore, if structural principles similar to those of Gothic architecture exist in literature, it is in the medieval arts of poetry that we may expect to find them. However, first, Frankl's theory of Gothic architecture will be outlined.

GOTHIC ARCHITECTURE

An attempt to illuminate the structural features of the Vulgate Cycle of Arthurian romance by means of a comparison with Gothic architecture of the same period demands an architectural terminology that both clearly describes Gothic architecture itself and that is also sufficiently abstract to lend itself to translation into a literary mode. Theories designed to account for the artistic phenomenon of Gothic cathedrals have proliferated since these churches first appeared, including Abbot Suger's statements regarding the meaning of his own church, St. Denis.[13] Many of these theories are useless to anyone wishing to understand the structural principles embodied in Gothic architecture, since they focus on elements other than the architecture, taking as a frame of reference something external to it.[14] However, development of the Gothic style in architecture is clearly presented by Paul Frankl in *The Gothic:*

Literary Sources and Interpretations Through Eight Centuries and *Gothic Architecture*.[15]

According to Frankl, Gothic style is characterized by the principles of Spatial Division, the Smooth Flow of Forces, and Diagonality; together these result in a style of Partiality. He contrasts this with the Romanesque style of Totality, in which he includes the principles of Spatial Addition, the Opposition of Forces (alternatively called Structure), and Frontality.[16] Frankl sees the transition from Romanesque to Gothic in stylistic terms and thus bases his definition of Gothic architecture on a purely descriptive analysis of the forms of individual architectural members categorized according to abstract stylistic concepts. By this method he seeks to arrive at a definition that includes everything that is Gothic and nothing else. Yet far from being reductive, his definition clarifies formal concepts by including monuments that often suffer from their attachment to concepts not essential to Gothic. For example, English Gothic architecture has a horizontal emphasis, but Frankl's definition can include it, since the definition does not contain the idea of verticality. Similarly, the features that do define Gothic architecture are limited very precisely by Frankl so as not to include any non-Gothic buildings; hence, plasticity cannot define Gothic, since it is also a characteristic of Renaissance and Baroque architecture.

The Gothic style of Partiality originated in and was based on the diagonal rib. When the first rib was introduced in a Romanesque structure, the rib participating in the principles of the Gothic disturbed the Romanesque style; "it opened the way towards a style of full *partiality* in which the parts would no longer be sub-wholes but *fragments*."[17] The introduction of the rib left two choices: the rib could be renounced for the sake of the Romanesque style of Totality, or "one could keep the rib because of the precision of its curvature and, in obedience to its divisional character, transform all Romanesque members until they conformed to the character of the rib."[18] Frankl's entire theory rests on this basis; by succeeding steps the Gothic style tended more and more toward Partiality in order to make the rest of the structure conform to the rib.

It is necessary to emphasize that these terms are used aesthetically to describe the impression made by the forms, rather than genetically to describe the process by which they were invented. "The question is not how the figure is *produced*, but of what it *consists*."[19] This distinction is especially important in the case of the concept of Division, as opposed to Addition. "From a purely *geometrical* point of view the figures are *different* but not opposite. *Aesthetically*, however, they are not merely different but also *opposites*."[20] The aesthetic impression received from viewing the high vault of a Gothic cathedral is that it consists of parts rather than of sub-wholes; parts by definition cannot stand alone or exist independently but are dependent members of a larger whole. Thus, any structure whose units of construction appear to be partial gives the impression of Division, even though it is obvious that these parts were of necessity added to one another rather than actually divided off from an original whole. The parts of a Gothic cathedral, once the process of construction is completed, appear to be divided from each other even though they are essentially indivisible. They are indivisible in the sense that they are completely dependent upon each other; but if they were not parts, incomplete and fragmentary parts, they would appear divisible and able to stand on their own. This for Frankl is the difference between a Romanesque and a Gothic cathedral. In a Romanesque cathedral every part, such as each bay, appears to be total in itself and added to the rest, upon which it does not depend (see figure 1); in a Gothic cathedral every part, again such as each bay, even if it is actually complete in itself, appears to be only fragmentary and unable to exist independently of the rest (see figure 2).

The concept of Diagonality further clarifies what Frankl means by Division. Diagonality is opposed to Frontality in the sense that in a Romanesque church one is confronted by structural members that one faces frontally. One may, of course, move to the side and see right angles, but even in this position one realizes that the structure, though no longer facing, is still frontal (see figures 1 and 3). Gothic architecture in its completed phase uses all diagonal members; the rib is the most obvious example, but this is true of the other members also. The piers are set diagonally so that a corner projects into the nave; and later in the Gothic period, the piers are covered with shafts so that one does not know where the front is (see figure 4). The proliferation of rounded and pear-shaped profiles and surfaces makes it impossible to confront any part of the structure frontally; at any given point one finds diagonal views (see figure 5).

Diagonality by its very nature is divisive rather than additive; it divides space but also lets space flow past, contributing to the impression of Partiality and interdependence. For example, the rib is placed diagonally and is also diagonal in its cross-section, having either a pointed or rounded—but never square—profile (see figure 6). Thus, it is divisive, looking in two directions; it partakes of both sides yet divides them. By contrast, in a Romanesque structure, which uses right angles and square profiles, each part appears whole in itself and contributes to the impression of Frontality (see figures 1 and 3). In a Romanesque cathedral one can always view the whole, or at least an independent sub-whole which produces the sense of completeness; whereas in a Gothic cathedral, because of diagonal forms and therefore necessarily oblique views, one is never in visual control of the entirety but forever sees only fragments.

According to Frankl, the other formal concept necessary to a definition of the style of Partiality is the Smooth Flow of Forces, as opposed to Romanesque Opposition of Forces, or Structure. He states, "The term structure is used to denote any system of building where members keep each other in balance under pressure and counter pressure. In structures every member is a whole and within the wholeness of the building it is . . . a sub-whole."[21] While this is necessarily true of all buildings in order that they stand, it is not always true aesthetically. The most obvious example of aesthetic Structure is found in the Greek temple where the colonnade obviously supports the· pediment which presses down upon it. The members of a Gothic cathedral, however, appear to operate on the principle of a Smooth Flow of Forces, not a dependency on

Fig. 1.   Trani, Ognissanti. Portico, general view.

Fig. 2.   Amiens Cathedral. Interior; vaults of last bay of nave, crossing, and choir.

Fig. 3.   Fontgombault Abbey. South bay of choir and part of south transept.

Fig. 4.   Bourges Cathedral. View from northwest end, showing partial elevation of nave and first south aisle.

Fig. 5. Bourges Cathedral. General view from northeast end, showing first north aisle and elevation of nave.

Fig. 6. Reims Cathedral. Interior, general view of lower gallery towards south aisle.

Fig. 7. Reims Cathedral. Interior, general view of crossing and nave from triforium of east end.

material pressure and counter-pressure; although the thrust of the high nave vaults is supported by the heavy pier buttresses on the exterior of the building, the aesthetic effect on the interior is one of uninterrupted upward soaring. Each part seems to flow into the next (see figure 7).

The impression of the Smooth Flow of Forces is enhanced by the other elements of the style of Partiality already discussed: Division and Diagonality. Parts flow into each other by means of diagonal members that participate in both sides of the element or space divided. These members implement the "smooth flow" from one part to the next, while at the same time stating the Partiality of each section. The Smooth Flow of Forces obviously increases the impression of Partiality, since it is an aspect of the interdependence of parts.

The value of Frankl's theory for literary study lies in its descriptive emphasis. He provides a set of concepts and a terminology that can illuminate the structural aspects of the literature written in the period of Gothic architecture. It is not unreasonable to expect the formal elements of two contemporaneous artistic achievements to exhibit numerous similarities. For an analysis of a literary form that continues to elude definition, Frankl's conceptual framework is potentially a valuable guide to that form's underlying aesthetic principles.[22] Adopting his theory as a source of meaningful structural terminology, one may attempt to identify the formal peculiarities of the thirteenth-century French Vulgate Cycle.[23]

ADAPTATION

Medieval literary art is the art of adaptation.[24] Medieval romancers not only use and adapt sources but are at pains to make clear that they are doing so. Romance references to sources are legion. In numerous cases the sources are identifiable; years of source study have yielded much valuable information about origins, analogies, and lines of transmission. From these studies we have learned that "invention" to the medieval author meant, in part, the finding of a story to adapt. However, whether or not an actual source for a work has been located, it is clear that medieval authors were eager to keep their audiences aware of the fact that they were using sources; they made reminders of this either in order to verify their own works' authenticity or to signal the improvements they made on received material.

Medieval literary adaptation involves recasting a given story according to the author's own point of view or according to his understanding of what the material ought to say. The medieval author found the means to accomplish this purpose in the arts of poetry written in the twelfth and thirteenth centuries. For the present discussion, it is sufficient to observe that Geoffrey of Vinsauf's dictum to lengthen what is short, shorten what is long—that is, to use the devices of amplification and abbreviation—could serve to produce a new version of the source by emphasizing latent features in it. This is what happens in all medieval romance.[25]

The supreme example of adaptation in the Middle Ages is the story of the Grail. As it passes through Chrétien and Robert de Boron to the Didot *Perceval*, the *Perlesvaus*, and the *Perceval* continuations, the structure of the quest(s) and the representation of the Grail undergo widely divergent treatments. All of these variations are unique responses to the same material and as such are significant examples of authorial intention imposing itself on a source; hence, they are adaptations. Yet, we can best approach adaptation in the Grail story by comparing works where it is known that one is the direct source of the other. Malory adapted the thirteenth-century *Queste del Saint Graal* in his *Tale of the Sankgreal*. Because in this case we have a recognized source,[26] a comparative study of the two works can illuminate for us the procedures of medieval romance art as adaptation.

Medieval Rhetoric

The twelfth and thirteenth centuries saw the composition of over a half-dozen arts of poetry, from Matthew of Vendôme before 1175 to John of Garland after 1229.[27] "Properly approached, these *artes* can afford us valuable clues about the

tools most readily available to the medieval poet and his purpose in using them."[28] During the Middle Ages "the world
had its rules; poetry had its rules. Technique was considered
teachable and was not dismissed as merely mechanical."[29]
Technique was, in fact, art. Among the authors of these treatises, Geoffrey of Vinsauf, writing about 1210, was the best
known. Over two hundred manuscripts of the *Poetria Nova*
have survived, far more than for any other rhetorical
manual.[30] Because of Geoffrey's popularity as well as his systematic presentation of instruction in composition, the *Poetria
Nova* will be used in this study as representative of what such
arts of poetry taught.

Geoffrey stresses the importance of invention in his architectural metaphor. The refashioning of found material was to
be accomplished by means of the tropes and figures the rhetorical manuals also contained. However, as is clear from the
emphasis Geoffrey and others place on careful conception of
the work, or on the "invention" of the new work in the mind
before actual writing, the separate rhetorical devices are subordinate to, yet essential for, the making of a new design out of
the *materia* the author has chosen to use.[31] Similarly, an
author's preconception of the work is meant to guide the
choice of natural or artificial order and the choice of the techniques of amplification or abbreviation. These elements of
disposition are always meant to support the author's initial
conception or invention of the work. Thus, in order to discover
the different intentions behind the *Queste* and Malory's *Sankgreal* and to understand the structural principles underlying
them, one can begin by analyzing the specific rhetorical devices the authors used to achieve their ends.

As Ernest Gallo comments, "Medieval poetics and medieval
poetry are both based upon rhetoric. . . . The same subject
matter will have different impacts, depending on presentation, manipulation, emphasis. Rhetoric teaches us not only
which facts to choose but also how to present them."[32] The
rhetorical devices chosen by an author to present his story will
determine its impact on his audience; these devices are not
confined to the sentence or the line of verse but pervade the

entire work in the form of the artful arrangement of larger narrative units.[33] This is evident partly in the medieval distinction, blurred though it was,[34] between grammar and rhetoric. The former is exemplified by Matthew of Vendôme's treatise, which deals specifically with the line of verse and is directed at less advanced students.[35] The surviving rhetorical manuals themselves, however, include the invention and disposition of material, thus indicating the applicability of their devices to larger narrative units. For example, although artificial order is often illustrated in the disposition of the parts of a single sentence, the plot structure of the *Aeneid*, since it begins *in medias res*, is used by Bernard Silvester and others as an example of artificial order.[36] So, too, in a medieval commentary on Horace, the word *iunctura* is made to fit a variety of contexts, "whether arrangement and disposition of narrative material . . . or arrangement and disposition of words and phrases in the sentence."[37] The adaptability of terminology to different levels or phases of composition is implied by other writers as well: "It is evident not only from the passage in Conrad of Mure, but also from Eberhard of Bethune's *Graecismus* that similar principles governed the choice and arrangement of different parts of the sentence and different parts of the plot. Eberhard uses Horace's instruction in the *Art of Poetry* regarding faults in narrative structure to criticize bad syntax."[38]

Furthermore, in the *Documentum de modo et arte dictandi et versificandi*, Geoffrey's discussion of digression as a means of treating an old subject with originality implies that digression as a rhetorical figure is not meant to be confined to the sentence.[39] Digression is in fact a characteristic feature of medieval romance; therefore, it should not surprise us if other devices taught in the schools from the rhetorical manuals were made to apply to the composition of entire works. As Professor Vinaver points out, the requirement that pupils comment upon chosen examples of Latin literature produced "a habit of mind which in a writer could easily become a habit of conception."[40] And he continues, "Rhetoric could thus lead to a purposeful refashioning of traditional material, and the adaptor could become to all intents and purposes an original author, except that, unlike some authors, he would care above all for the *way* in which he told his stories and measure his achievement in terms of such new significance as he was able to confer upon an existing body of facts."[41] Adaptation of material in accord with authorial intention was the heart of medieval writing, and the school instruction in rhetoric is the means by which it was achieved. As Gallo states, school exercises could be mechanical, but "the decisive factor will be not the tool but the genius of the man who commands it."[42]

The devices most obviously used by thirteenth-century writers of French romance are the techniques for amplification. The vast Vulgate Cycle of Arthurian romance is an expansion of hitherto separate and sometimes undeveloped themes. This proliferation of narrative is related to Geoffrey of Vinsauf's advice in his *Documentum* for treating old material: "The first mode [for treating familiar material] is that we do not delay where others delay; but, where they delay, let us go on; where they go on, let us delay."[43] More relevant, however, is the relationship of amplification and abbreviation to the structural principles underlying Gothic architecture as described by Frankl.

Before we pursue the analogy, however, it is well to remind ourselves that the analogy does not presuppose equivalence or cause and effect. As Vinaver states in another context, it "should not be taken as evidence of a common origin, still less of an influence of one form of art upon another. The object of the comparison is simply to clarify, by mere juxtaposition, the processes at work in two parallel spheres of artistic activity."[44] It is likely, however, that writers living in the time when Gothic cathedrals were rising in France would choose, from the compositional techniques they had been taught, those that corresponded to the aesthetic common around them. A comparison of Gothic architecture and thirteenth-century French Arthurian romance, then, although not demonstrating the influence of one art upon another, can illuminate the structural aspects of one work of art by means of another. Because Frankl's study has provided a structural terminology for Gothic architecture and because a structural language to describe thirteenth-century romance is still lacking, his work can serve as a useful guide to thirteenth-century structural aesthetics.

The Queste and Amplification

As we have seen, Frankl describes Gothic architecture by means of a system of abstract concepts: it is a style of Partiality, a style composed of the structural principles of Division, Diagonality, and the Smooth Flow of Forces. The impression produced by a style of Partiality is that of a proliferation of fragmentary but interdependent parts. Those techniques for amplification in the arts of poetry that best describe the *Queste* also produce a style of Partiality by serving to elaborate descriptive features of the ultimately ineffable Grail. Care must be taken, however, to distinguish between the two sets of concepts—Frankl's description of Gothic architecture and the rhetorical techniques for amplification. The former is a twentieth-century formulation of structural principles designed to describe all Gothic architecture. The latter is medieval literary theory meant to teach students good writing but not necessarily meant to result in a style of Partiality. The fact that the use of principles derived from rhetorical theory results in such a style in the *Queste* is very likely a consequence both of the contemporaneity of the art forms and of the religious mystery which both the *Queste* and Gothic architecture were meant to express. The *Queste* can be described by means of three techniques for amplification that most obviously define its structure and that also correspond in a mutually illuminating way to the three structural principles equalling a style of Partiality. Because the arts of poetry generally list a variable number of techniques for amplification—always more than three—[45] the parallels to be described in this study are not meant to imply that we are dealing with equivalent systems. Nonetheless, the amplificatory devices making up the structure of the *Queste*, like the structural principles on which Gothic architecture is based, do lead to a style of Partiality.

The first principle described by Frankl as contributing to the style of Partiality is spatial Division. This means that once the cathedral is complete, each structural element of it appears to be a division or "part" of a larger whole; the parts do not appear to have been added to each other. The impression of spatial Division is caused by the apparently fragmentary and incomplete nature of the members making up the whole. If these members were independent, they would appear to be added to each other by accumulation of parts; they would not depend on the whole for their integrity. The equivalent principle in the arts of poetry is *interpretatio* (repetition): "Let one and the same thing be concealed under multiple forms—be varied and yet the same" (*PN*, p. 24).[46] Utilizing this principle in literary composition would mean that the same "thing"—idea or meaning—would be "divided" in order to be presented in various manifestations. The manifestations would then become the "parts" from which the whole is to be implied. Like the elements of a Gothic cathedral, these parts do not appear to be juxtaposed to one another, for they are interdependent; they are not complete in themselves because their meaning depends on the whole, the "same thing." They may be incremental, pointing toward the whole that is never completely contained in any one of them except partially. This principle is used by Alain de Lille when he has Nature express the essences of earth and of the human body: "For just as, of the four elements, the concordant discord, the single plurality, dissonant consonance, the dissenting agreement, produce the structures of the palace of earth, so, of four ingredients, the similar unsimilarity, the unequal equality, the unformed conformity, the separate identity, firmly erect the building of the human body."[47] This example illustrates syntactic repetition in description. The principle often operates for narrative as well.

Because of the predominence of diagonal members in a Gothic cathedral, views are necessarily oblique and incomplete; one is never able to perceive the whole but at any one point sees only fragments. This principle, Diagonality, is paralleled in the arts of poetry by *circumlocutio*: "Do not unveil the thing fully but suggest it by hints. Do not let your words move straight onward through the subject, but, circling, take a long and winding path around what you were going to say briefly" (*PN*, p. 24).[48] Circumlocution of the kind recommended by Geoffrey results in diagonal views, since at any point in the work, the "subject" will fall outside the main line of immediate vision; the "long and winding path" will prevent its being presented directly. Vision will also be fragmentary and incomplete because, while circling the subject, the narrative will take the form of hints which are partial. The diagonal quality of *circumlocutio* is evident in much medieval romance, including the Vulgate Cycle, where each section is introduced by an explicit statement marking the end of one section and the beginning of the next: "Mes a tant lesse ores li contes a parler d'aux et retorne a monseignor Boort de Gaunes"[49] [But here the tale leaves them and returns to Sir Bors of Gaunes (p. 175)]. This type of statement, including both parts, underscores both the fragmentary nature of the sections and their interdependence. Thus, the views produced by a work based on the principle of *circumlocutio* are also oblique. For any given section the whole, the meaning, is seen from an angle—that is, from a particular perspective; furthermore, the other sections are seen this way as well. And since the "hints" are sections, not separate stories, they are incomplete parts making up the whole and thus contribute to the realization of structural Partiality.

The final structural principle by which Frankl defines the style of Partiality is the Smooth Flow of Forces, defined as the aesthetic effect of part flowing smoothly into part with no apparent dependence on structural thrust and counter-thrust. The structural elements of a Gothic cathedral appear to soar freely, no longer subject to physical laws. Correspondingly, *digressio* permits the author to proceed beyond the dictates of immediate probability:

. . . go outside the bounds of the subject and withdraw from it a little; let the pen digress, but not so widely that it will be difficult to find the way back. . . . A kind of digression is made when I turn aside from the material at hand, bringing in what is actually remote and altering the natural order. (*PN*, p. 35)[50]

Digressio releases the author from the restrictions of time and place, since it accommodates that which is remote and thus allows for the free flow of the temporal and spatial dimensions. *Digressio* also contributes to partial structure; each digression is not complete in itself but is a division of a whole, to whose meaning it contributes. These varied manifestations of a single subject, like the parts produced by *interpretatio* and *circumlocutio*, are interdependent, since as digressions they increase our understanding of the whole yet are incomplete in themselves and depend on a smooth return to the subject matter.

Thus, the medieval arts of poetry offer traditional literary devices that parallel the formal concepts by which Frankl describes Gothic architecture. Partiality itself can be understood as a form of extended *synecdoche*, a metaphorical mode that Geoffrey defines thus: "suppressing the whole . . . imply that whole from the parts" (*PN*, p. 53).[51] A literary work utilizing these compositional principles would provide a meaningful structural parallel to Gothic architecture. The contemporaneity of Gothic architecture and the Vulgate Cycle of Arthurian romance supports an investigation of the comparison. The precision of Frankl's terminology for architectural structure derives from the necessity for the art historian to read a "language of stone"; in architecture meaning is arrived at primarily through structure. Because of the continued use of the analogy between architecture and literature throughout the Middle Ages and the prevalence of the compositional techniques encouraged in the arts of poetry, the principles described by Frankl, translated into literary terminology found in contemporary poetic treatises deriving from traditional rhetoric, reveal the structural language of the *Queste del Saint Graal*.

Malory and Abbreviation

All the rhetorical devices used by the author of the *Queste* are means to lengthen a work, but amplification was not Malory's intention in the *Sankgreal*, which is one-third the length of the *Queste*. Moreover, Caxton says that Malory's work is "reduced . . . into Englysshe," and Malory himself says that the *Sankgreal* is "breffly drawyn oute of Freynshe." The techniques of amplification which served to enlarge and elaborate the great prose romances of the thirteenth century were not used by Malory as compositional tools. However, he did not achieve a shorter work by simply telling half the story or by leaving out a large number of adventures; Malory relates the story as he finds it in the *Queste*, using the same exemplary knights whose sections and adventures follow each other in the same order as they do in his source. Therefore, it is necessary to determine the principles controlling Malory's excisions and minor additions, and to analyze these before attempting to identify his intent. The medieval arts of poetry provide a useful terminology under the topic of abbreviation.

Geoffrey of Vinsauf describes abbreviation as follows: "If you wish to be brief, first prune away those devices mentioned above which contribute to an elaborate style; let the entire theme be confined within narrow limits. . . . Let *emphasis* be spokesman, saying much in few words. . . . Give no quarter to *repetition*. Let skillful *implication* convey the unsaid in the said. . . . Let the craftman's skill effect a *fusion of many concepts in one*, so that many may be seen in a single glance of the mind" (*PN*, pp. 40–41).[52] Geoffrey goes on to say that abbreviation is used "not to enshroud facts discreetly in mist, but rather to clear away mist and usher in sunlight" (*PN*, p. 41).[53] These precepts obviously are directed not merely at shortening a work; they also provide compositional principles for a particular kind of work, one that is direct rather than circuitous, straightforward rather than digressive, immediate rather than interpretive. They provide for a work that is not repetitious, digressive, or ambiguous. In a word, it is based on Totality rather than Partiality.

Throughout Paul Frankl's work, the principle of Partiality in architecture is defined in opposition to the style of Totality as represented in Romanesque architecture. The style of Totality is characterized by Addition, Frontality, and Structure, or

Opposition of Forces. Such principles are analogous to Geoffrey's conception of abbreviation. They are presented here with the intention of clarifying the "shape" of a literary work composed according to his instructions for abbreviation and to illustrate the real differences that exist between such a work and one whose structure is predicated on Partiality. Of course, Gothic architecture and the Vulgate Cycle are contemporaneous, whereas Romanesque architecture and Malory are not. Therefore, no attempt is being made to find actual analogies between Malory's work and Romanesque architecture; instead, the general description of Totality can serve to illustrate the structure toward which Malory tended by his systematic movement away from a style of Partiality.

In a study of Renaissance architecture, written before his work on Gothic, Frankl sets out principles describing architecture of the period 1420–1550.[54] Many of the features he finds to be characteristic of this architecture are identical to those he later uses to describe Romanesque architecture; and in fact many of the same terms are used, such as "addition" and "frontality." Furthermore, in a brief mention of Renaissance structure in *Gothic Architecture*,[55] Frankl refers to it as a style of Totality. And, of course, early Renaissance architecture is contemporary with Malory. However, because Frankl's discussion of the opposing principles of Totality and Partiality is most systematic in his description of Gothic and Romanesque architecture, and because his work generally assumes a kind of alternation or pendulum swing between these principles, Romanesque and Gothic will be used to delineate the structures of the *Queste* and the *Sankgreal*.

The movement toward Totality in Malory's work can be usefully described using the principles of abbreviation. However, Geoffrey's instructions on abbreviation do not lend themselves to exact definition, since they are less discursive than those for amplification. For example, to "prune away those devices mentioned above which contribute to an elaborate style" is a broad dictum and can certainly be understood through a knowledge of amplificatory devices; but it is negative and hardly a specific device in itself. Furthermore, because of the general nature of Geoffrey's advice, the various means used by Malory to abbreviate his work overlap with each other more than amplificatory devices do in the French and are thus less readily identifiable.

Of course, Malory is no more contemporaneous with Geoffrey of Vinsauf and the other writers of the arts of poetry than he is with Romanesque architecture, although manuscripts of these treatises were still in existence. But it is not necessary to believe that Malory learned abbreviation from these works, for by the time he was writing, abbreviation was common among writers of romance, and particularly in England.[56] The long interlaced romance cycles had already been and were still being broken up and shortened. Therefore, Malory was not the first to use abbreviation; nonetheless, a careful analysis of the *Sankgreal* in the light of rhetorical abbreviation does reveal these principles as he used them to adapt the story of the Grail in accordance with his own understanding of it.

In the *Queste* and in the *Sankgreal*, amplification and abbreviation function both statically and dynamically.[57] Static amplification and abbreviation are description and refer to the Grail as object, while dynamic amplification and abbreviation are the narrative produced by the Grail and refer to the quests of separate knights for it. However, although the rhetorical terminology is the same whether a specific device is illustrated statically or dynamically, the specific application requires some distinction. For instance, whereas dynamic *digressio* as narrative in the *Queste* amplifies the work by means of large narrative sections set in the distant past, static *digressio* as description expands the Grail's meaning by any verbal reference to its history prior to Arthur. Static and dynamic *circumlocutio* are even more divergent. When used statically to describe the Grail, *circumlocutio* fits Geoffrey of Vinsauf's synonym for it: paraphrase. However, when used dynamically as narrative, it corresponds to the image Geoffrey uses in representing its function as part of amplification, where it is "the long and winding path" of narrative quests conforming to a central meaning.

Varying images for the same terminology are also found in

the static and dynamic abbreviation of the *Sankgreal*. For example, one of Geoffrey's devices for abbreviation is the elimination of repetition. For static description of the Grail as object, Malory eliminates the epithets referring to the Grail in the *Queste* which repeat its meaning on various levels; it is a purely verbal use of the device. Dynamically, however, elimination of repetition requires the deletion of entire sermons from the narrative, sermons that repeat the meanings of events on a discursive level. The following chapters demonstrate how the *Queste* and Malory's *Sankgreal* use the static and dynamic rhetorical principles underlying their respective structural elaborations.

CHAPTER II

The Grail in the
Queste and Malory

The subject of both the *Queste del Saint Graal* and Malory's *Sankgreal* is the Grail itself; where it appears miraculous events occur, and it produces narrative in the form of quests for it. From Chrétien de Troyes and Robert de Boron in the twelfth century, the Grail has exerted a fascination on the imagination and functioned as a spiritual symbol in a variety of works. The way it was represented in each serves as a guide to the idea, the "invention," by which each succeeding author understood the Grail story as *materia*.

The specific rhetorical devices illustrated in the *Queste* and Malory for describing and referring to the Grail are too dense for systematic distinction of each in the discussion that follows, even though they are present and loosely indicated. Although these devices are considered separately in the following chapters on narrative in the *Queste* and in the *Sankgreal*, in the discussion of static representation of the Grail, they are best understood as features of larger concepts. For the *Queste* they function as elements of *synecdoche*, the metaphorical mode by which is derived the "whole from the parts" (*PN*, p.

53); for Malory they fall under the general heading of *emphasis*, "saying much in few words" (*PN*, p. 40).

In the *Queste* the total meaning of the Grail lies behind the phenomena that constitute its partial manifestations. Varied references to and appearances of the Grail represent partial reflections of that meaning. But the Grail and its meaning remain ultimately ineffable in their entirety. The static amplification by which the *Queste* describes the Grail relies on the three devices for amplification discussed above: *interpretatio*, *digressio* and *circumlocutio*. Through *interpretatio* the meaning of the Grail is presented in multiple forms; its total meaning is said to remain the same, but the representations of it vary. *Digressio* introduces manifestations of the Grail from earlier historical periods, using temporal juxtaposition to suggest significance. *Circumlocutio*, verbal paraphrase, reveals meaning obliquely through narrative elaboration. Geoffrey of Vinsauf sums up his instruction on amplification: "In this way, plentiful harvest springs from a little seed; great rivers draw their source from a tiny spring; from a slender twig a great tree rises and spreads" (*PN*, p. 40).[1] In the *Queste del Saint Graal* the seed is the Grail; it produces the work, and the structure of the work ultimately defines it, by means of amplification. The task the author of the *Queste* sets himself is to unveil partially, through romance, manifestations of the Grail's essence.

Although Malory shows great respect for his source, the changes he makes in the description of the Grail are significant. He consistently narrows and concretizes references to it in order to make what in his source is ineffable into something simple which we can know fully. He consistently attempts to restrict description of the Grail to what is appropriate for the Eucharistic vessel. The very amplificatory devices used by the *Queste* author to represent his conception of the Grail are those Malory eliminates in representing his own. We will begin by examining the descriptions of and references to the Grail in the French *Queste*, and follow that with an analysis of Malory's adaptation of his source.

STATIC AMPLIFICATION AND THE GRAIL

Critical opinion is divided as to what the Grail in the *Queste* is or signifies; it has variously been identified as a symbol of God, Grace, or the Eucharist.[2] Each of these designations is made on the basis of good evidence, since each is used to describe the Grail in the *Queste*. But it is wrong to reduce the spectrum of significance to one of these meanings, especially since in most instances where the Grail is mentioned, one of these designations appears alongside many others. This suggests that the Grail is defined periphrastically, with each mention of it demonstrating a valid feature of its whole meaning. The appearances of or specific references to the Grail in the *Queste* fall into three general categories: first, the epithets or synonyms applied to it; second, the verbs used to describe what one is to do with it or what it does; and third, the statements of its ineffability, particularly from those who have achieved it. Besides specific references, the meaning of the Grail is also presented through historical digressions of a tropological, exemplary, or prophetic kind. These digressions reveal more and more of the historical significance of the Grail, until history and present achievement merge in the final Grail scenes.

The first appearance of the Grail is at Arthur's court on Pentecost Sunday, where those present "fussent enluminé de la grace dou Saint Esperit" (p. 15, l. 13) [were all illumined . . . by the grace of the Holy Ghost (p. 43)]. It distributes to each knight seated at the Round Table whatever food ("viande," p. 15, l. 27 [p. 44]) he desires; after the Grail vanishes, all thank God for filling them "de la grace dou Saint Vessel" (p. 15, l. 33 [p. 44]). This is the first conjunction of the attributes of grace and food, a combination repeated and amplified throughout the *Queste*. After the Grail's departure, Nascien's messenger addresses the court, introducing the notion of ineffability to connote its essence: to him who is successful on the quest will be revealed "ce que cuers mortex ne porroit penser ne langue d'ome terrien deviser" (p. 19, ll. 25–26) [that which the heart of man could not conceive nor tongue relate (p. 47)]. Galahad will echo these words in the final vision of the Grail that precedes his passing away (p. 278, ll. 4–5 [p. 283]).

The Grail appears again in the first Lancelot section where Lancelot's inability to respond to it is a sign of his fallen state. Here it also demonstrates the power to heal; when the sick knight kisses it, he says "Ha! Diex, gariz sui!" (p. 59, ll. 17–18) [Ah! God, I am healed! (p. 83)]. Then he, and Lancelot soon after him, vow to discover the truth of the Holy Grail. When Lancelot is reproved by the voice of God, he knows "qu'il a falli a savoir la verite del Saint Graal" (p. 61, ll. 24–25) [(he had failed to pierce the secret of the Holy Grail (p. 85)], and laments his blindness "que je ne pui veoir chose qui de par Dieu soit" (p. 62, ll. 2–3) [that I could not discern the things of God (p. 85)]. Both of these verbs ("savoir," "veoir") are conjoined frequently in the *Queste* to indicate the goal of the seeker of the Grail; the quest will not be achieved until the Grail is seen and known. For the most part, however, these verbs differ with regard to the range of their objects: "veoir" usually has a narrow range that is directed at God's secrets, or, as Lancelot says in the example above, the things of God; "savoir" tends to have a more general range of objects that includes the Grail but also some of the Grail history, the Lance, the adventures of Logres, and the theological truths the Grail stands for. This is the sense in which the healed knight uses "savoir" (p. 60, ll. 26–30 [p. 84]), as it is also that of Perceval's aunt when she is giving Perceval instructions for his quest (p. 78, ll. 28–31 [p. 101]). We shall see that by the time Galahad has truly "seen" the Grail, historical manifestations as *digressio* have been revealed to him so that he also "knows" it.

Until the final Grail ceremonies, *interpretatio* (repetition) and *digressio* extend and deepen the characteristics of the Grail; by repeated amplification we are brought closer to an understanding of it. For example, in the early *Queste* sections, Perceval is told by a priest that when King Crudel held Joseph of Arimathea's son in prison, they had the Grail with them and therefore "il ne doutoient rien de chose qui a la viande corporel covenist" (p. 84, ll. 5–6) [whose presence left them carefree for their bodies' food (p. 105)]. Similarly, the Grail enabled twelve loaves to feed more than four thousand of Joseph's people (p. 75, ll. 18–26 [p. 98]); moreover, the presence of the Grail sustained most of these by "grace" (p. 83, l. 32 [p. 105]). Lancelot is told by a hermit that the quest was undertaken to "savoir aucune chose des merveilles dou Saint Graal" (p. 116, ll. 8–9) [glean some knowledge of the mysteries of the Holy Grail (p. 134)]. Later another priest informs him that he would not see ("veoir" p. 123, l. 7 [p. 140]) the Grail even if it were before his eyes. Afterwards the same priest explains the Grail table to Lancelot by the Parable of the Wedding Feast; this is the table "ou li preudome mengeront" (p. 128, l. 8) [where the worthy men . . . shall be fed (p. 145)] at the end of the quest, thus extending the "viande" image. The idea of "seeing" recurs when another hermit, while interpreting Lancelot's dream and wishing to demonstrate Nascien's worthiness, explains that "Nostre Sires li lessa veoir les granz secrez et les granz repostailles del Saint Graal" (p. 134, ll. 29–30) [Our Lord vouchsafed to him the vision of the high secrets and the mysteries of the Holy Grail (p. 151)].

In the next series of references to the Grail, which occurs in the hermit's interpretation of Hector's and Gawain's dreams, and in the priest's initial injunction to Bors as he begins his quest, the range of meanings for the Grail becomes more complex. The hermit tells Gawain and Hector that Perceval and Galahad will not leave the Grail, "car il troveront tant doulcor en la viande dou Saint Graal" (p. 157, l. 25) [for the food of the Holy Grail will be so sweet to them (p. 171)], but that Hector and Gawain will never find it; that is, "les secrees choses Nostre Seignor" (p. 158, l. 10) [the mysteries of Our Lord (p. 172)]. Here the Grail is referred to as both "viande" and as receptacle for "secrees choses." The hermit explains Lancelot's Grail experience by saying that the knight will almost drink from the "spring" that never fails: "ce est li Sainz Graax, ce est la grace del Saint Esperit" (p. 159, ll. 1–2) [it is the Holy Grail, the grace of the Holy Ghost (p. 172)]. Here the attributes attaching to the Grail have become more complex; different meanings occur in such close proximity that they begin to merge in mixed metaphors: Lancelot will kneel down "por boivre et por estre rasaziez de sa grant grace" (p. 159, ll. 12–13) [to drink his fill of its abounding grace (p. 173)]. And Bors is told by the priest that those who are worthy will receive "la viande del Saint Graal, qui est repessement a l'ame et sostenement dou cors" (p. 163, ll. 6–7) [the food of the Holy Grail which fills the soul to overflowing and sustains the body too (p. 176)]. Thus the metaphors of eating and drinking the "viande" of the Grail—suggesting the Eucharist—merge with the idea of grace.

The varied images and meanings attached to the Grail converge still further during the three Grail ceremonies. Lancelot's experience of it is one of "seeing": he sees the Grail, the angels, the priest. When the priest elevates the host, "il fu avis a Lancelot que desus les mains au preudome en haut avoit trois homes, dont li dui metoient le plus juene entre les mains au provoire; et il le levoit en haut, si fesoit semblant qu'il le mostrast au pueple" (p. 255, ll. 22–25) [Lancelot thought he saw, above his outstretched hands, three men, two of whom were placing the youngest in the hands of the priest who raised him aloft as though he were showing him to the people (p. 262)]. The Trinity is thus shown to the people, but communion does not take place, at least not before Lancelot falls into his twenty-four-day trance. When Lancelot awakens from this trance, he describes his blissful experience as an ineffable vision: "Je ai . . . veu si granz merveilles et si granz beneurtez que ma langue nel vos porroit mie descovrir, ne mes cuers meismes nel porroit mie penser, com grant chose ce est. Car ce n'a mie esté chose terriane, mes esperitel" (p. 258, ll. 6–10) [I have seen . . . such glories and felicity that my tongue could never reveal their magnitude, nor could my heart conceive it. For this was no earthly but a heavenly vision (p. 264)]. The emphasis on "vision" in Lancelot's Grail experience is pertinent to his efforts to overcome spiritual blindness; but it also demonstrates that "seeing" is among the true Grail experiences, while stressing anew the ineffability of the vision. Besides these features of the Grail, Lancelot's experience includes a Grail feast, during which "li Sainz Graax ot ja raemplies les tables si merveilleusement que greignor plenté ne poist penser nus hom" (p. 259, ll. 28–29) [the Holy Grail had already loaded the tables with such a wealth of dishes that a more plenteous spread were past imagining (p. 266)]. Thus, Lancelot "sees" but does not partake of a Grail feast that has Eucharistic overtones, yet he *does* partake of "viande" provided by the Grail at a feast that is not Eucharistic. The meaning of the Grail thus remains elusive but suggestive. We, as readers, enjoy only partial understanding.

The second Grail ceremony, which takes place at the Castle of Corbenic and in which Galahad, Perceval and Bors participate, has a largely Eucharistic character. Josephus, the first Christian bishop, descends from heaven and administers the mass. He takes bread from the Grail, into which enters from above the figure of a child. He then places the bread back in the Grail and tells the assembled knights that because they have struggled to see ("veoir") the mysteries of the Grail, "si seroiz repeu de la plus haute viande et de la meillor dont onques chevalier gostassent, et de la main meesme de vostre Sauveor" (p. 269, ll. 27–29) [you shall be filled with the most sublime and glorious food that ever knights have tasted, and this at your Savior's hand (p. 275)]. The crucified Christ then emerges from the Grail and speaks:

Mi chevalier et mi serjant et mi loial fil, qui en mortel vie estes devenu esperitel, qui m'avez tant quis que je ne me puis plus vers vos celer, il covient que vos veoiz partie de mes repostailles et de mes secrez, car vos avez tant fet que vos estes assis a ma table, ou onques mes chevaliers ne menja puis le tens Joseph d'Arymacie. Mes del remanant ont il eu ausi come serjant ont: ce est a dire que li chevalier de çaienz et maint autre ont esté repeu de la grace del saint Vessel; mais il n'ont mie esté a meesmes ausi come vos estes orendroit. Or tenez et recevez la haute viande que vos avez si lonc tens desirree, et por quoi vos estes tant travailliez. (p. 270, ll. 5–16)

[My knights, my servants and my faithful sons who have attained to the spiritual life whilst in the flesh, you who have sought me so diligently that I can hide myself from you no longer, it is right you should see some part of my secrets and my mysteries, for your labours have won a place for you at my table, where no knight has eaten since the days of Joseph of Arimathea. As for the rest, they have had the servant's due: which means that the knights of this castle and many more beside have been filled with the grace of the Holy Vessel, but never face to face as you are now. Take now and eat of the precious food that you have craved so long and for which you have endured so many trials. (p. 276)]

The qualities associated with the Grail converge here in Christ's words and blend to make its meaning more mysterious. But mystery in the Middle Ages is a blend of both mystery in the modern sense and of signification.[3] Because all the amplified attributes—secrets, grace, "viande"—have accompanied the Grail's appearances in the *Queste*, and because its truths have been partially revealed to us and to the questing knights by *circumlocutio*, we partially "know" the Grail. Had this statement of Christ's appeared earlier in the work, it would have seemed nonsense; however, because we have learned with the knights, we understand. Christ next gives the host to the knights and tells Galahad, "Or as veu ce que tu as tant desirré a veoir, et ce que tu as covoitié. Mes encor ne l'as tu pas veu si apertement com tu le verras" (p. 270, l. 33–p. 271, l. 2) [Now hast thou seen the object of thy heart's most fervent longing; yet shalt thou see it plainer still one day (p. 276)]. The place where Galahad is to see the secrets of the Grail more clearly is the spiritual palace at Sarras; God sends him there with the Grail, which leaves Logres because the people there are wicked, even though they have been sustained "de la grace de cest saint Vessel" (p. 271, ll. 9–10) [by the grace of the Holy Vessel (p. 277)].

While the three elect knights accompany the Grail to Sarras, Perceval hears Galahad pray that he might die when he chooses. When Perceval questions him about this, Galahad responds by describing his experience of the Grail ceremony discussed above: "en cel point que je vi ces aferes que cuers de terrien home ne porroit penser ne langue descrire, fu mes cuers en si grant soatume et en si grant joie que se je fusse maintenant trespassez de cest siecle, je sai bien que onques hom en si grant beneurté ne morut com je feisse lors" (p. 274, ll. 12–17) [in the moment that revealed to me those things that the heart of mortal man cannot conceive nor tongue relate, my heart was ravished with such joy and bliss, that had I died forthwith I know that no man ever breathed his last in such beatitude as then was mine (p. 279)]. Thus Galahad again expresses the ineffability of the Grail; to him was revealed what the heart of man cannot think nor tongue describe, and in this state of spiritual bliss he wishes to leave this world, "en voiant les merveilles del Saint Graal" (p. 274, ll. 25–26) [while looking on the glories of the Holy Grail (p. 280)]. While viewing it, he is "translatez de la terrienne vie en la celestial" (p. 274, ll. 19–20) [translated in that moment from the earthly plane to the celestial (p. 280)].

The final Grail ceremony is the granting of Galahad's prayer. He has endured two years of purification through suffering: first, in prison, where he was sustained by the Grail; and then as ruler of Sarras, always waiting to be released from life. At this last ceremony, Josephus calls Galahad forward and says, "verras ce que tu as tant desirré a veoir" (p. 277, ll. 31–32) [look on that which you have so ardently desired to see (p. 283)]. Galahad trembles at the sight of the "esperitex choses" (p. 278, l. 2) [spiritual mysteries (p. 283)]. He looks to heaven and exclaims, "Sire, toi ador ge et merci de ce que tu m'as acompli mon desirrier, car ore voi ge tot apertement ce que langue ne porroit descrire ne cuer penser. Ici voi ge la començaille des granz hardemenz et l'achoison des proeces; ici voi ge les merveilles de totes autres merveilles!" (p. 278, ll. 3–7) [Lord, I worship Thee and give Thee thanks that Thou hast granted my desire, for now I see revealed what tongue could not relate, nor heart conceive. Here is the source of valour undismayed, the springhead of endeavour; here I see the wonder that passes every other! (p. 283)]. When Galahad sees the mysteries of the Grail revealed "apertement," we are still not told explicitly what they are; Galahad praises God for unveiling for him what can never be told, but the truth of the Grail is revealed to us even here only by its effects. Galahad receives the host from the hand of Josephus—who takes it from the table, not from the Grail—and then, as he was promised, dies. The last we see of the Grail is its removal to heaven by a hand come down to take it; as the author says, since that time, "il ne fu puis hons si hardiz qu'il osast dire qu'il eust veu le Seint Graal" (p. 279, ll. 6–7) [no man since has ever dared to say he saw the Holy Grail (p. 284)].

As the discussion above has shown, the essence of the Grail in the *Queste* is its mystery; to identify it specifically is to ignore the diversity of its manifestations and the interpenetration of images attached to it. Since even those who achieve it—and especially Galahad, who sees it openly and directly revealed—cannot express what they see, it is obvious that its truths are ineffable and ultimately inexpressable. Galahad, at the moment he sees the Grail secrets revealed, is transported to heaven; one cannot be illuminated with that bright light and continue in mortal life. The author has shown us the Grail, but his admitted inability to define it totally or to describe it concretely suggests it would be presumption on our part to attempt to do so. The truth of the Grail is adumbrated. We know all we can of it through the partial views provided by each device. The hand comes from heaven to remove the Grail; beyond what the author has told us, we can say and see no more.

STATIC ABBREVIATION AND THE GRAIL

Analysis of the Grail as object in the French *Queste* shows that it cannot be specifically identified with God, grace, or the Eucharistic vessel, although it contains features of each. It represents God's secrets, and so it remains hidden to all except Galahad, who, upon seeing these secrets *apertement*, is received into heaven. The references to the Grail and the attributes applied to it emphasize the elusiveness of any single definition: metaphors are mixed, and the Grail contains seemingly contradictory qualities at one and the same time. The entire narrative thus unveils gradually the myriad manifestations of the Grail itself, while circumscribing it by means of men's responses to its manifestations until we discover all we can know of it—only a partial knowledge.

Although Malory retains some of the variety of the French in his representation, he tends to narrow the spectrum more specifically to the Eucharistic vessel.[4] This process eliminates the gradual revelation of the ineffability of the Grail. This change in meaning for the whole work will be dealt with later; for the present it is necessary to analyze the changes Malory makes in the *Queste's* representation of the Grail.

Its first appearance in Malory, as in the *Queste*, is at Arthur's court on Pentecost Sunday. The details of the incident are the same—the Grail appears, borne by no hand, accompanied by sweet fragrances; and all those present receive the food they most desire. But the assembled knights, besides being struck dumb, look at each other "and eyther saw other, by their semynge, fayrer than ever they were before" (p. 865, ll. 22–23). This phrase is not in the *Queste*, and it introduces a theme alien to that work but stressed by Malory throughout, that of brotherhood. By emphasizing the ideal relationship of the sworn brotherhood of the Round Table at the first appearance of the Grail, Malory adumbrates his identification of worthiness to achieve the Grail with true chivalry, which for him includes brotherhood.[5] After the disappearance of the Grail in this scene, those present thank God—in the *Queste* for filling them "de la grace dou Saint Vessel" (p. 15, l. 33) [with the grace of the Holy Vessel (p. 44)], in Malory "of Hys good grace that He had sente them" (p. 865, ll. 35–36). The change here is minor, but Malory's version does preclude the identification of the Grail itself with grace and so attenuates the accretion of meanings to the Grail found in the French.

Other changes Malory makes in this episode serve the same purpose. He eliminates another passage in the French linking grace with the Grail (Q. p. 16, ll. 10–11 [p. 44]); and whereas in the *Queste*, Gawain says the knights were unable to see the Grail when it was present because they were so beguiled ("engignié," Q. p. 16, l. 16 [p. 44]), Malory attributes their blindness to the fact that "hit was so preciously coverde" (M. p. 866, ll. 5–6). When Gawain in the *Queste* vows to go in search of the Grail, he says, "ne ne revendrai a cort por chose qui aviegne devant que je l'aie veu plus apertement qu'il ne m'a ci esté demostrez, s'il puet estre en nule maniere que je lou puisse veoir ne doie" (Q. p. 16, ll. 21–24) [nor will I return to court, come what may, until I have looked openly upon the mystery we have but glimpsed this day, provided that I am capable and worthy of such grace (p. 44)]. This implies both that to see the Grail openly is more than simply seeing it with one's eyes and that in order to see it, a certain degree of worthiness is necessary.[6] However, at this point, Malory's Gawain vows, "and never shall I returne unto the courte agayne tylle I have sene hit more opynly than hit hath bene shewed here" (M. p. 866, ll. 9–11). Here Gawain's statement appears to refer to the fact that the Grail was "so preciously coverde."

The old man who enters the court to tell the knights that they may not take maids or ladies with them on this quest concludes his speech thus in the *Queste*:

Car ceste Queste n'est mie queste de terriennes choses, ainz doit estre li encerchemenz des grans secrez et des privetez Nostre Seignor et des grans repostailles que li Hauz Mestres mostrera apertement au boneure chevalier qu'il a esleu a son serjant entre les autres chevaliers terriens, a qui il mostrera les granz merveilles dou Saint Graal, et fera veoir ce que cuers mortex ne porroit penser ne langue d'ome terrien deviser. (Q. p. 19, ll. 19–26)

[For this is no search for earthly things but a seeking out of the mysteries and hidden sweets of Our Lord, and the divine secrets which the most high Master will disclose to that blessed knight whom He has chosen for His servant from among the ranks of chivalry: he to whom He will show the marvels of the Holy Grail, and reveal that which the heart of man could not conceive nor tongue relate. (p. 47)]

In the corresponding place in Malory, he says, "For I warne you playne, he that ys nat clene of hys synnes he shall nat se the mysteryes of oure Lorde Jesu Cryste" (M. p. 869, ll. 3–4). Malory has eliminated the statement that this quest is not for "terrienes" things, and although he uses the word "mysteryes," it does not render fully "grans secrez," "privitez," "grans repostailles," and "granz merveilles." Malory obviously considered the various appellations given to the object of the quest in the French too various and diffuse, and so "reduced" them in Caxton's expression to the mysteries of Christ, conventionally regarded as His body and blood in the Eucharist.

Malory's intention of presenting the Grail more concretely than his source, thus divested of much of its mystery, is also apparent in his elimination of the last sentence in the passage above from the *Queste*; there we are told specifically that whoever achieves the quest will see what mortal heart cannot think nor earthly tongue tell. Malory's excision indicates that he does not mean to present the Grail as ineffable; rather, what he chooses to keep of the passage represents the Grail as available to human sight and understanding. The final significant change in this passage concerns the requirements for achieving the Grail. Malory's "clene of hys synnes" corresponds to the French "netoiez et espurgiez de totes vilanies et de toz pechiés mortex" (Q. p. 19, ll. 18–19) [cleansed of grievous sin and purged of every wickedness (p. 47)], but Malory eliminates the statement that the Grail will be revealed only to the "boneuré chevalier qu'il a esleu a son serjant entre les autres chevaliers terriens." Thus, Malory removes the intimation of predestination found in his source, making the Grail experience potentially available to any knight who is "clene of hys synnes." This is in keeping with what we have learned so far of Malory's altered conception of the Grail itself; if the Grail is the Eucharistic vessel, not ineffable but accessible to human experience, it follows that knowledge of the Eucharist is possible for every man who lives a good Christian life. Near the end of the episode at Arthur's court in the French, each knight who sets out on the quest takes an oath on holy relics not to return to court "devant qu'il la verité savroit del Saint Graal" (Q. p. 23, l. 20) [until he learned the truth about the Holy Grail (p. 50)]. Malory leaves out the oath, probably because it indicates that the knights are in search of that which cannot be known, a conception that does not suit his presentation of the Grail.

The Grail's next appearance is in the first Lancelot section when Lancelot is unable to respond to its presence and the sick knight is healed. Malory follows broadly his source for this incident but makes some significant alterations in details. Whereas in the *Queste* the sick knight kisses the silver table supporting the Grail (Q. p. 59, ll. 15–16 [p. 83]), in Malory he "towched the holy vessell and kyst hit" (M. p. 894, l. 30), an action, as Vinaver rightly notes, that would be impossible in the French.[7] However, Malory's consistent concretization of the Grail, his reduction of mysterious and symbolic features, allows such a gesture.[8] Malory's attempt to narrow the range of the Grail's meaning is even more apparent in the other change he makes in this scene. The sick knight's prayer for healing in the *Queste* begins, "Biau sire Diex, qui de cest Saint Vessel que je voi ci venir avez fet tant bel miracle en cest pais et en autre" (Q. p. 59, ll. 7–9) [Gracious Lord God, who through this Holy Vessel that I now set eyes on hast performed so many miracles in this and other lands (p. 83)]. In Malory, however, the knight says, "Fayre swete Lorde whych ys here within the holy vessell . . . " (M. p. 894, ll. 27–28). From a vessel through which God has worked miracles in many lands, the Grail becomes in Malory the vessel containing Christ. Such specificity is never found in the *Queste*, for in that work the entire narrative is a product of the gradual unveiling of what man can partially know of the meaning of the Grail. Malory, in contrast, is clearly establishing a specific meaning for the Grail from the beginning, one that is readily understood in Eucharistic terms.

The next extended reference to the Grail in the *Queste* occurs in the Perceval section when the history of King Mordrain is related to Perceval by a monk. All of these Grail references are omitted by Malory, and the digressive history itself greatly reduced; however, in view of what we have seen of his conception of the Grail, these excisions are quite understandable. The Grail causes Joseph of Arimathea's people to subsist on grace alone when in Britain (Q. p. 83, ll. 29–33 [p. 105]); it is ineffable, yet it literally feeds them. Malory compresses the entire story of King Mordrain and says succinctly of Mordrain's overwhelming desire to approach the Grail that "ever he was bysy to be thereas the Sankgreall was" (M. p. 908, ll.

20–21), a bare statement that suppresses attributes altogether.

In the second Lancelot section, Malory again leaves out many references to the Grail. It is true that in the *Queste* these references are made in passing, included as parts of sermons that Malory radically reduces; nonetheless, the exclusion of most of the Grail references is significant, for they present the Grail in various contexts, a manner Malory systematically eschews. Malory leaves out the hermit's sermon to Lancelot at the beginning of the section and thus his reference to "merveilles dou Saint Graal" (Q. p. 116, ll. 8–9) [mysteries of the Holy Grail (p. 134)]. He retains the admonition of another hermit when Lancelot says he is seeking the Grail: "Well, . . . seke ye hit ye may well, but thoughe hit were here ye shall have no power to se hit, no more than a blynde man that sholde se a bryght swerde" (M. p. 927, ll. 12–14). This is a close rendering of the French (Q. p. 123, ll. 5–8 [p. 140]). However, Malory omits the hermit's statement that had Lancelot not been so steeped in sin, he would not have been "avugle devant la face ton Seigner" (Q. p. 126, l. 33) [blinded in the presence of your Lord (p. 144)], an indication that the Grail manifests God. He also drops the hermit's allegorical interpretation of the Parable of the Wedding Feast, wherein the Wedding Feast is seen as the Table of the Holy Grail at which all true knights shall be fed (Q. p. 128, ll. 6–15 [p. 145]). Similarly, in the hermit's interpretation of Lancelot's dream of his lineage, Malory omits the fact that God allowed Nascien to see "les granz secrez et les granz repostailles del Saint Graal" (Q. p. 134, ll. 29–30) [the high secrets and the mysteries of the Holy Grail (p. 151)]. Hence, all references to the Grail wherein its nature is not clearly defined, or at least not presented as readily accessible to human understanding, are left out by Malory.

The next significant Grail reference in the *Queste* is the beautiful, complex allegory of the fountain given in the hermit's explanation of Lancelot's role in Hector's dream. In the French the fountain is the Grail, the grace of the Holy Ghost, the gentle rain, and the Gospel's sweet words all at one and the same time; it is then called specifically "la grace del Saint

Graal'' (Q. p. 159, ll. 5–6 [p. 172]). Yet when Lancelot comes before it to drink of this grace, the spring, the Grail, hides itself; thus, the images attached to the Grail here are thoroughly intermingled, causing it to elude definition and specificity. Malory's rendition of this description is as follows:

And the welle whereat the watir sanke frome hym whan he sholde have takyn thereoff? (And whan he saw he myght nat have hit he returned from whens he cam, for the welle betokenyth the hyghe grace of God; for the more men desyre hit to take hit, the more shall be their desire.) So whan he cam nyghe the Sankgreall he meked hym so that he hylde hym nat the man worthy to be so nyghe the holy vessell, for he had be so defoyled in dedly synne by the space of many yere. Yett whan he kneled downe to drynke of the welle, there he saw grete provydence of the Sankgreall. (M. p. 947, ll. 19–28)

Although the pattern of narration in the two works is similar, Malory, besides eliminating many of the images associated with the Grail in the French (''la douce pluie,'' ''la douce parole de l'Evangile'' [the gentle rain, the Gospel's dulcet words]), tends to separate the Grail from the image he does retain. He keeps the idea of grace, but in his version of the passage, the grace of God and the Grail itself are two separate things; Malory finds in his source ''la grace del Saint Graal,'' and with the clear purpose of disjoining the two notions, places the ''grace of God'' and the ''Sankgreall'' in separate sentences, where they are obviously not meant to be the same thing. He does appear to *link* the well and the Grail in the last sentence (''Yett whan he kneled downe to drynke of the welle, there he saw grete provydence of the Sankgreall''), but they are not seen as two manifestations of the same thing.

In the *Queste* another ambiguous, or rather polyreferential, description of the Grail occurs in the context of the priest's exhortations to Bors concerning the requirements for achieving the Grail, a lengthy sermon (Q. p. 162, l. 19–p. 164, l. 7 [pp. 175–77]), which Malory reduces to four lines (M. p. 955, ll. 11–14) by eliminating all mention of the Grail. Here again, the attributes attached to the Grail in the *Queste* do not suit Malory's conception of it. The priest in the *Queste* explains that those who seek the Grail must transform their lives; they must confess and become clean knights for the sake of that which they seek. The image he applies to the Grail is that of "viande":

Car il lor a prestee la viande del Saint Graal, qui est repessement a l'ame et sostenement dou cors. Iceste viande est la douce viande dont il les a repeuz et dont il sostint si longuement le pueple Israhel es deserz. (Q. p. 163, ll. 6–9)

[For He has given them the food of the Holy Grail which fills the soul to overflowing and sustains the body too. This is the sweet food He has filled them with, even as He sustained the Israelites for so long in the desert. (p. 176)]

The priest goes on to say that "tout ausi come la viande terriane s'est changiee a la celestial" (Q. p. 163, ll. 11–12) [But just as the earthly food has been changed for that of heaven (p. 176)], so also must those seeking the Grail change their lives from earthly to heavenly. In this sermon, although the word "viande" in connection with the Grail may have Eucharistic implications, the image has a broader range of meaning than Malory intends for the Grail. The comparison between the "viande" and the manna that God sent the Israelites in the desert does not point to any special Eucharistic qualities in the Grail, and the other instances of "viande" are more metaphorical and symbolic than concrete. Hence, Malory's abbreviation of specific references to the Grail continues to follow a pattern resulting from his attempt to make it readily comprehensible.

Counter to Malory's consistent elimination of Grail references that do not suit his purpose, in the Bors section he adds one that further clarifies its meaning in his work. At the beginning of the section, Bors has an *avision:* he sees a pelican strike its own breast with its beak, dying so that its young may be brought back to life by the spilling of their parent bird's blood (Q. p. 167, l. 31–p. 168, l. 14 [p. 181]). In the *Queste* the abbot interprets this vision as an allegory of the Redemption (Q. p. 184, ll. 5–30 [pp. 196–97]). Malory mostly follows this interpretation but adds a reference to the Grail: "there was the tokyn and the lyknesse of the Sankgreall that appered afore you, for the blood that the grete fowle bledde reysyd the chykyns from dethe to lyff" (M. p. 967, ll. 9–11). Here Malory connects the Grail with the spilled blood of Christ, a connection again suggesting that Malory sees the Grail as the Eucharistic vessel.

The episode of the hart and the four lions, in which Galahad, Bors and Perceval see the hart become Christ and the lions transformed into the four evangelist symbols, is presented in both the *Queste* and Malory as a Grail adventure, one that signifies that these three knights will achieve the Grail. The adventure is a symbolic vision revealing the doctrines of the Incarnation, Passion, and Resurrection. In both works the ability of the three knights to penetrate this vision is marvelled at by the priest and indicates to him that they are worthy of carrying the quest to its end. The difference between the two works lies in the *Queste*'s emphasis on this adventure as actually containing a partial revelation of that which is sought, and Malory's emphasis on the adventure as foreshadowing the revelations to come. In the *Queste* the priest says to the knights, "vos estes cil a qui Nostre Sires a mostrez ses secrez et ses repostailles" (Q. p. 235, ll. 30–31) [For to you has Our Lord revealed His secrets and His hidden mysteries (p. 244)]. God has clearly revealed secret things to them. The priest also points out that no other knight has ever penetrated the truth of this mystery (Q. p. 236, ll. 13–15 [pp. 244–45]). Then Galahad, Bors, and Perceval, weeping for joy, thank God "de ce qu'il lor a ceste chose mostree apertement" (Q. p. 236, ll. 23–24) [for allowing them to see His truth unveiled (p. 245)]. In Malory the priest welcomes the knights and says, "ye bene they unto whom oure Lorde shall shew grete secretis" (M. p. 999, ll. 26–27). There is no indication in his words that this adventure has any more bearing on the Grail quest than to demonstrate the worthiness of the knights; it is not itself, as it is in the *Queste*, a partial revelation of the truth of the Grail. For Malory the "grete secretis" that are to be revealed abide in the truth of the Eucharist; hence, those adventures that express further aspects of the Grail are adapted to this end. What in the *Queste is* a Grail adventure has become in Malory a *prediction* of Grail adventures.

Malory's treatment of the final Grail appearances during the Grail ceremonies at Corbenic and Sarras follows the *Queste* quite closely; these ceremonies have a largely Eucharistic character in the *Queste*, and Malory needs only to leave out those elements that impede a strictly Eucharistic interpretation of the Grail. Lancelot's partial achievement of the Grail at Corbenic is left virtually intact, since during this episode the Eucharistic mystery is enacted and Christ bodily appears at the consecration of the host (Q. p. 255, l. 14–p. 256, l. 11 [pp. 262–63]; M. p. 1015, l. 24–p. 1016, l. 15). This episode in the *Queste* contains nothing to contradict Malory's conception of the Grail, and therefore he closely translates his source.

Similarly, the Grail ceremony at Corbenic in which Galahad, Perceval, and Bors participate is left relatively unchanged by Malory. As in the *Queste*, Josephus, the first Christian bishop, officiates at the service and then vanishes as Christ, bearing the signs of the passion, appears from out of the Grail to take his place. Malory does, however, significantly reduce Christ's words to the assembled knights (Q. p. 270, ll. 5–16 [p. 276]). He eliminates the reference to the days of Joseph of Arimathea and also does not mention "la grace del saint Vessel":

My knyghtes and my servauntes and my trew chyldren which bene com oute of dedly lyff into the spirituall lyff, I woll no lenger cover me frome you, but ye shall se now a parte of my secretes and of my hydde thynges. Now holdith and ressyvith the hyghe order and mete whych ye have so much desired (M. p. 1030, ll. 6–11).

Malory's elimination of any reference to Joseph of Arimathea confines the significance of the episode to the present moment, and his deletion of the notion of grace removes any ambiguity of meaning surrounding the Grail. It is clear that for Malory "my secretes" and "my hydde thynges" indicate the Eucharist for, as in the *Queste*, his version goes on to describe Christ distributing the host from the Grail: "Than toke He hymselff the holy vessell and cam to sir Galahad. And he kneled adowne and resseyved hys Saveoure" (M. p. 1030, ll. 12–13). Here Malory found in the *Queste* what he wanted to say.

Malory's conception of this incident is indicated by his changes in the response Galahad makes when Perceval asks him why he prays to be allowed to die at the moment he chooses. In the *Queste* Galahad's response is a lengthy statement of the ineffability of the Grail's meaning (Q. p. 274, ll. 8–26 [pp. 279–80]). He explains that he wishes to find again the bliss he has experienced and thus desires to die while gazing on the "merveilles del Saint Graal" (Q. p. 274, ll. 25–26) [glories of the Holy Grail (p. 280)]. For Malory, who views the Grail in equally religious although less mystical terms, this must not seem a sufficient reward for a saintly life, especially since his Grail is available on earth to all good men. Thus his Galahad wishes to die, not in order to gaze again on the mysteries of the Grail but because his soul "shall be in grete joy to se the Blyssed Trinité every day and the majesté of oure Lorde Jesu Cryste" (M. p. 1032, ll. 23–24). Malory has thus shifted the emphasis and significance of this scene as well as of the work itself. In the French *Queste* the goal of every knight is to see the Grail *apertement*, but since man in his mortal state can achieve only partial insight into the Grail's meaning, it is appropriate that Galahad wishes to die while gazing on its mysteries, for only through death can he attain complete understanding and vision. Because the French author's Grail is a complex symbol, including not only the persons of the Trinity but many other aspects of spiritual reality besides, he would never, as Malory does, have Galahad say that he wished to die so he may see "the Blyssed Trinité every day." However, Malory's Galahad can express this goal, since for Malory worthiness to partake of the Eucharist should obviously be rewarded by entry into a conventional heaven where one could be near the Trinity "every day."

The final Grail scene, in which Galahad gazes inside the Grail, receives the Lord's body from Josephus, and then dies, is largely unaltered by Malory. The episode is Eucharistic in character, and Malory changes the few significant details that detract from this interpretation. In both works Galahad's body is seized by trembling upon contemplation of the spiritual mysteries, and he then prays (Q. p. 278, ll. 3–12 [p. 283]). Malory reduces this prayer greatly; his Galahad says, "Lorde, I thanke The, for now I se that that hath be my desire many a day. Now, my Blyssed Lorde, I wold nat lyve in this wrecched worlde no lenger, if hit myght please The, Lorde" (M. p. 1034, ll. 24–27). Malory again leaves out Galahad's statement that he has seen what cannot be expressed, since this negates his conception of the Grail as comprehensible. He also eliminates Galahad's description of what he has seen as the source of all prowess and endeavor, and as the marvel of all marvels, because these attributes broaden the Grail's meaning beyond the presentation Malory means to give it.

Finally, in the French Josephus takes the *Corpus Domini* from the table—not the Grail—and gives it to Galahad. In Malory the table is not mentioned; rather he writes, "And therewith the good man toke oure Lordes Body betwyxte hys hondis, and profird hit to sir Galahad, and he resseyved hit ryght gladly and mekely" (M. p. 1034, ll. 28–30). Although Malory does not specifically say that "oure Lordes Body" is taken from the Grail, the context of the gesture, as well as Malory's general direction in his previous alterations of Grail references, permits the interpretation that this is what occurs. The episode is thus a consistent, coherent conclusion to Malory's adaptation of the Grail story. Whereas in the *Queste* the goal of the knights is to become worthy to see and understand the meaning of the Grail—hence Galahad's final Grail experience is one of gazing on its mysteries, mysteries that no one can see face to face and continue in earthly life—the goal in Malory is to lead a life worthy of partaking of the true Eucharist which is contained in the Grail. In each work the goal is ultimately achieved by Galahad, and in Malory as well as in the *Queste* the Grail is taken to heaven by a mysterious hand; "And sythen was there never man so hardy to sey that he hade seyne the Sankgreal" (M. p. 1035, ll. 20–21).

The author of the French *Queste* describes the Grail by

means of amplification; he elaborates its attributes and thus its meaning, allowing only partial insights, in order to show forth its ineffability. Malory, by contrast, eliminates all elaboration of the Grail's meaning which does not correspond to his intended representation of it as Eucharistic vessel. The compositional principle Malory used to adapt the *Queste* to his own conception of the Grail is clearly that of abbreviation. He does so in a manner consonant with Geoffrey of Vinsauf's dictum to "prune away those devices . . . which contribute to an elaborate style; let the entire theme be confined within narrow limits" (*PN*, p. 40). The devices Malory prunes away are those used in the *Queste* to amplify the meaning of the Grail: *interpretatio, digressio,* and *circumlocutio.* By eliminating *interpretatio,* he leaves out all the varied ways to say one and the same thing, the incremental repetition that in the *Queste* serves to broaden and diffuse the meaning of the Grail. He also sharply abbreviates *digressio* by removing a great number of references to the Grail during the time of Joseph of Arimathea. By doing so, he narrows the concept of the Grail in time, thus placing direct emphasis upon its specific meaning at the present Arthurian moment. Finally, he eliminates *circumlocutio,*[9] the proliferation of images, ideas, and objects that in the *Queste* leads to partial knowledge of the Grail and to an awareness of its ineffability. By making clear from the beginning that the Grail is to be identified with the Eucharistic vessel, Malory eliminates the need for a plethora of attributes pointing to this knowledge.

The argument that Malory narrows his definition of the Grail to the Eucharistic vessel is not meant to imply that his conception of the Grail is a totally integrated one. For example, if the Grail is simply the vessel used in the Mass, then why the quest for it; and conversely, if it is a kind of archetypal Eucharistic vessel, how can one say it is available to all men? Even more disconcerting, if it is indeed available to all worthy men, what happens to the worthy men of Logres when the Grail is received into heaven? In spite of these difficulties, Malory's direction appears clear: he very systematically eliminates those attributes that make the French Grail ineffable, and in so doing he presents the Grail as meaningful within the context of the Eucharist and thus as a more human goal than the Grail of the *Queste*. The avoidance of amplificatory devices in Malory's description of the Grail effectively confines his theme to narrower limits than those found in his source. The use of abbreviation has allowed him to adapt his source to his own intention. Geoffrey says that abbreviation may be used to "clear away mist and usher in sunlight"; Malory, by that device, clears away the mists surrounding an ineffable Grail and allows us to see it as comprehensible and attainable by good men.

CHAPTER III

Dynamic Amplification: Narrative and Meaning in *La Queste del Saint Graal*

Through static amplification as description, the author of the *Queste* demonstrates the ineffability of the Grail. Through varied descriptions of the Grail as object and through specific references to it, he shows that the vessel's essence lies in its mystery. However, the author also presents the Grail's ineffability through dynamic amplification as narrative. Narrative in the *Queste* is produced by the Grail's effects on those who go in search of it, and their responses to the vessel itself. When the Grail appears in Arthur's court and then disappears, a quest is undertaken by the knights to find it. Thus, the Grail causes the narrative that follows that incident.

The structure of the *Queste del Saint Graal* can be usefully described in terms of the style of Partiality. The impression this narrative structure presents is not that of a monolithic totality, but rather of partial views and oblique vistas; we are constantly confronted with parts of adventures and experiences whose core remains obscure. Despite the obvious religious intent of the *Queste*, it is also a romance of chivalry, firmly set in the *Lancelot-Grail* cycle of which it is a part.[1] However, the religious purpose, the visible demonstration of the secrets of God, determines the way in which the parts of the story are ordered and arranged.[2] Rather than simply multiply adventures on a horizontal plane, the author of the *Queste* uses the rhetorical techniques of amplification to reveal in parts the central truth of his story, the meaning of the Grail. Thus, besides marking horizontal, chronological units, his narrative divisions also move the story vertically through allegory among various levels of significance. This narrative amplification of the Grail in the *Queste* is presented in parts conforming to the *synecdochic* mode and hence to structural partiality. The amplificatory devices used by the author to effect partial views are, as for the Grail itself, *interpretatio, circumlocutio,* and *digressio.*

Interpretatio

Geoffrey of Vinsauf's *Poetria Nova* defines *interpretatio* (repetition) as follows: "let one and the same thing be concealed under multiple forms—be varied and yet the same" (*PN*, p. 24). The use of repetition, presenting the same idea or thought in a number of ways, necessarily results in a story divided into parts; and in the case of the *Queste*, they are equal, fragmentary, and interdependent parts, like the structural elements of a Gothic cathedral. In the sections devoted to each knight, his spiritual progress in the quest—or lack of it—is divided into episodes reproducing his experience on varying levels: real history, visions, and dreams. Although repetition is one of the major means of amplification in the *Queste*—each knight's adventures to some extent mirroring those of the others, whether by similarity or opposition—its use can best be illustrated within the adventures of a single knight. Bors's experience in the quest will serve to demonstrate how within the large sections of the plot, the horizontal divisions of which are determined mainly by change of character, the story is vertically fragmented, as it were, even further.

The appearance of the Grail in Arthur's kingdom effects a near reversal of all formerly accepted values: earthly prowess is no longer sufficient and in fact, rather than proving one's knightly worthiness, may only reveal his sins. Therefore, each knight's understanding of *chevalerie celestielle* must be demonstrated through experience "concealed under multiple forms" that are "varied and yet the same." Adventures in the *Queste* come only to those who are worthy. They function as tests, the achievement of which means that a knight will be granted further adventures as manifestations of the Grail. Since Bors is one of the three elect knights, he does consistently meet with meaningful adventures.

At the beginning of his section, Bors meets a priest who counsels him on the spiritual condition proper for one who wants to succeed in the quest (p. 163, ll. 11–17 [p. 176]). Patience and humility are required of a knight, rather than prowess in arms. Bors does the right thing by asking the priest to hear his confession, and the priest asks him as a penance to wear a white shirt and to take only bread and water until he is seated at the table of the Holy Grail—to all of which Bors readily agrees. What Bors has been told here is that if he does penance, he *will* sit at the Grail table. But since he is concerned with learning to do right, he does not hear the prediction. He does, however, prove his understanding of the priest's distinction between "terrien" and "celestiel" when he says of the bread that the priest holds in Mass:

Je voi que vos tenez mon Sauveor et ma redemption en semblance de pain; et en tel maniere nel veisse je pas, mes mi oil, que sont si terrien qu'il ne pueent veoir les esperitex choses, nel me lessent autrement veoir, ainz m'en tolent la veraie semblance. (p. 167, ll. 4–8)

[I see that you are holding my Savior and Redeemer under the guise of bread. I should not be looking on Him in this wise were it not that my eyes, being mortal clay, and thus unapt to discern the things of the spirit, do not permit my seeing Him any other way, but rather cloak his true appearance. (p. 180)]

Thus, Bors demonstrates both his humility and his awareness that the "veraie semblance" of Christ is inaccessible to earthly sinners. This episode, on the level of real history, functions as a parallel to the last scene in this section, the explanation of his adventures by the good abbot. Bors's experience is framed by spiritual instructions initially and spiritual explanation finally. Nonetheless, these didactic statements of significance are only parts of Bors's adventures; although explicit, they are no more or less meaningful than the visions, dreams, and adventures granted him. Although the priest's instructions contain everything Bors needs to know and do in order to succeed in his quest, it is only knowledge. Bors must still come to understand through his adventures the significance of that knowledge. The fact that Bors invariably, almost automatically, does the right thing in all his adventures is less the result of the priest's instructions than of the knight's own spiritual condition. He acts rightly because he is virtuous; he is not virtuous because of his actions, as in the pre-*Queste* Arthurian world.

Upon leaving the priest and setting out on his quest, Bors soon experiences an *aventure*: he witnesses the great bird that dies for its young by tearing open its own breast with its beak and letting the blood flow onto its young, who revive through the parent bird's death. Although this episode occurs on the level of real narrative history, as does Bors's meeting with the priest, it is figurally significant and takes on the character of a vision or a dream. Furthermore, in the special world of the *Queste*, this vision is referred to as an "aventure" (p. 168, l. 8); in that world only events that are spiritually meaningful qualify as *aventure*, as evidenced by Gawain's complaint elsewhere that although he has killed many knights, he has had no adventure.[3] Since a knight's response to an event together with his spiritual worthiness determine whether he will have an adventure, two knights may encounter the same set of circumstances, and for one it will be an adventure and for the other it will not.[4] Thus, the fact that Bors's encounter is called an *aventure* although he is merely a passive observer, and that he is granted this *aventure* at the very outset of his quest, is an important indication of his spiritual preparedness for the quest.

Just as Bors did not actively seek the adventure but passively had it appear to him, so he cannot interpret it for himself, even though he recognizes it as meaningful:

Quant Boort voit ceste aventure, si se merveille trop que ce puet estre,
car il ne set quel chose puisse avenir de ceste semblance. Mes tant
conoist il bien que ce est senefiance merveilleuse. (p. 168, ll. 8–11)

[As Bors stood watching this phenomenon, he wondered, awe-
struck, what it signified, not knowing what reality might underlie the
form. He knew enough, however, to recognize it for a sign of great
significance. (p. 181)]

Although the episode is real and is comprehensible on the
literal level, it does have a deeper meaning that demands
explanation; because Bors is not capable of understanding it
alone, to him the phenomenon is incomplete and fragmentary, even though containing significance within itself. It does
not gain essential meaning from the abbot's explication later in
the section, although new significance for Bors is given to it at
that time. However, when the episode takes place, it is a
partial revelation of the meaning of the Grail as far as Bors is
able to respond to it, just as is the abbot's explanation itself.

Narrative elaboration by means of repetition becomes in-
creasingly complex and sophisticated with the next episode in
the Bors section. Within the framing incident, the battle with
Priadan le Noir—which itself is allegorical—Bors has two allegorical dreams that he cannot understand; one of them reverberates back on the framing incident, while the other gives
veiled indications of the proper actions to be taken by Bors in a
future episode. The Priadan le Noir episode itself, the story of
a lady beseiged in a tower and deprived of her lands by her
sister upon the death of *rois Amanz*, is typical of many situations in romance; there is little to indicate its allegorical nature,
and in fact its didactic meaning remains hidden until the good
abbot's explanation later. We discover then that on the allegorical level Bors, by undertaking to do battle for the lady, is
defending Holy Church; he is prepared to die on Christ's
behalf, just as in the great bird episode Christ revealed to Bors
the readiness with which He died for him. All this, however,
does not substantially affect the literal episode. Bors has adventures that he does not understand and which require
explanation by those qualified to do so, and these explanations

illuminate on a spiritual level all that has happened to him. But the adventures as Bors experiences them are valid on their own level, since his response is made on the basis of his own inadequate understanding but perfect virtue.

Bors has two dreams ("avision," p. 171, l. 14 [p. 184]) on the night before he is to defend the lady. In the first, two birds, one black and one white, both ask him to serve them; in the second, that of the two lilies and the rotten tree trunk, Bors is told that should the occasion arise where he must make a choice, he is to save the two lilies rather than the rotten wood. Again Bors recognizes the dreams as significant when he cannot interpret them (p. 172, ll. 1–3 [p. 184]). Although both bear on the literal narrative and pattern Bors's future actions, since he does not understand the dreams, he cannot yet choose to follow their instructions. But the truth that has been revealed to the knight actually resides within him, for even without understanding he will do what is right when the time comes. He is, as it were, programmed by his virtue. The dream of the birds refers to the battle of the next day: the black bird signifies the lady for whom he fights, who in turn is a symbol for the church, while the sisters also stand for the Old and New Law. The white bird, the swan who is white and fair on the outside and black within, is "l'anemi" (p. 185, ll. 30–31 [p. 198]), besides representing the Old Law and the older wicked sister. Bors, of course, has already chosen to fight on the right side when he has the dream, even though for him the significance of his choice is clear only from the abbot's explanation much later. In his second dream, Bors agrees to heed the advice to save the two lilies rather than the rotten tree trunk. Later, when the adventure referred to in the dream occurs, Bors does not recognize it as such; but he does preserve the purity of the young knight and maiden (the two lilies) rather than rescue his sinful brother, Lyonel (the rotten wood), from what appears to be certain death. The morning after these puzzling dreams, Bors defeats Priadan le Noir in a battle whose description recalls any number of other romance battles that are not allegorical. Thus, the Priadan le Noir episode begins and ends on the literal historical level.

This episode is an excellent example of the use of repetition for narrative elaboration; by means of literal history, vision, dreams, and the allegory of the framing episode, the author of the *Queste* has expressed on different levels a single message. The dreams that Bors has the night before his battle are repetitive elaboration, since they do not determine his actions; they simply state his forthcoming experience in another mode. Even when the complex allegories within allegory of this episode become clear in the abbot's explanation at the end, the relationships of these narrative parts remain mysterious, due to the lack of causal connections among them—the dreams do not *cause* the actions. Yet the interlacing of meaning on various narrative levels deepens and expands the significance of the episode as a whole, and this produces the impression of partial but interrelated revelations. The dreams depend on the actions and the actions on the dreams for their significance, but each is only a partial—yet complementary—facet of the truth of Bors's experience in the *Queste*. Morton Bloomfield has said of motivation in romance that "one is driven to assume that if he were to see events from above or from another center the inexplicable would be explicable."[5] In the *Queste* the center is God; since man can never see from His perspective, ultimate truth, which is one and whole, is divided and presented in parts through repetition on different levels: "multiple forms—varied and yet the same." Through *synecdoche* the whole is implicit and immanent in these parts.

Soon after the battle with Priadan le Noir, Bors comes upon the adventure referred to in his second dream, that of the two lilies and the rotten tree trunk. First, he sees his brother being beaten by two knights obviously intent on flailing him to death; just as Bors is about to rush to Lyonel's rescue, however, he hears from another direction cries of distress from a maiden being carried off by a knight just as obviously intent on ravishing her. The situation presents a seemingly insoluble dilemma, since it appears to Bors that his immediate assistance is required to save two different persons. His dream is of no help because he is not aware of the relationship of his dream to this adventure. Nonetheless, Bors chooses what seems to him the right thing to do and thus acts in conformity with his dream. As far as he is concerned, a knight cannot allow a maiden to be dishonored. He determines to rescue her while praying God to protect his brother.

After Bors rescues the maiden, the connection between this episode and the dream becomes clear to him, for as the maiden says, "Et s'il [her would-be ravisher] l'eust fet, il fust mors del pechié et honiz dou cors, et moi desennoree a toz jorz mes" (p. 176, ll. 26–28) [For had he gained his ends he would have forfeited his soul and suffered bodily hurt, and I should have been disgraced for evermore (p. 189)]. Thus, Bors has saved the innocence of both the knight and the lady; he made the right choice because, as the abbot later explains, he set Christian charity above natural love. The abbot also tells Bors that such an important adventure would not have come to him were he not worthy (p. 187, ll. 20–23 [p. 199]). Therefore, once again, although Bors was unaware of the connection between the adventure and the dream until the abbot's explanation, he acted out of the strength of his faith and virtue, and manifested on the level of narrative the truth of his dream.

Following this adventure is the false priest episode, which provides a new test of Bors's virtue and repeats, through a series of manifestations, the meaning of the truth symbolized by the Grail in relation to Bors. Bors encounters the false priest when he returns to where he had last seen Lionel. Although he does not recognize the priest as false, he does express some bewilderment when the priest takes him to a chapel, where the body Bors believes to be that of Lyonel can be properly buried—a chapel in which the knight can find neither holy water nor cross "ne nule veraie enseigne de Jhesucrist" (p. 178, l. 31 [nor veritable symbol of Jesus Christ (p. 191)]. However, Bors asks the priest to interpret the great bird episode and the two dreams, but the priest chooses to explain only the dream of the black and white birds. The white bird, he says, is a beautiful maiden who loves Bors and will die of grief if he rejects her love; the black bird is the sin that will cause him to reject her. And the false prophet asserts that Bors will refuse her love not from fear of God or by his own virtue but out of desire to be held chaste by the world and to win transitory glory. Further-more, this sin will have even worse results: Lancelot will be killed by the maiden's kinsmen, and so Bors will be in effect Lancelot's murderer as well as the murderer of the maiden. And according to the priest, Bors is a murderer already, since he could easily have saved from death his brother Lyonel, whose life was worth the virginity of every maiden in the world. Bors, who acts on faith and not reason, is speechless: "Quant Boort ot que cil en qui il cuidoit si grant bonté de vie le blasme de ce qu'il avoit fet de la pucele, si ne set que dire" (p. 179, ll. 30–32) [When he heard the man whom he took for a model of holy living condemn what he had done on the girl's behalf, Bors was lost for a reply (p. 192)].

When Bors is led to the tower where the beautiful maiden lives of whom the false priest spoke, she quickly declares her love and offers herself to the knight. Bors refuses under any circumstances to betray his vow of chastity. True to the false priest's prediction, the lady responds to Bors's refusal by throwing herself off the tower to her death. However, Bors makes the sign of the cross, and the truth of the episode becomes clear: "Maintenant ot entor lui si grant noise et si grant cri qu'il li est avis que tuit li anemi d'enfer soient entor lui"; and, the author adds, "sanz faille il en i avoit plusors" (p. 182, ll. 3–5) [Immediately he was enveloped in such a tumult and shrieking that it seemed to him that all the fiends of hell were round about him: and no doubt there were a number present (p. 194)]. The presence of the diabolic creatures makes Bors realize that he has narrowly escaped damnation and that he owes his rescue to faith in God. His understanding of the adventure is enhanced by the discovery that the body of his "dead brother" has disappeared. He concludes correctly that it was a phantom produced by the devil and that Lyonel may still be alive.

This episode within the Bors section, like the Priadan le Noir episode, contains further divisions corresponding to different modes of representation. On the one hand, Bors's encounter with the false priest is literal historical narrative; even though the priest is not a human being but "l'anemi," which gives the episode *senefiance* beyond that of the literal, the knight's meeting with him is nonetheless a literal adventure, not a dream or a vision. On the other hand, the false priest's explanation of the dream of the birds is ostensibly a doctrinal exposition—as are in fact the expositions provided by all of the priests, abbots, and holy men in the *Queste*—and as such takes place on the level of interpretation, even though in this case that interpretation is false. As such, it is part of the allegory; the false explanation contrasts with the truth embodied in the Grail.

The inclusion of this false explanation suggests the dangers inherent in the quest for the Grail for even the best knights. Bors's understanding of what is required in order to achieve the quest is tested, and he achieves the adventure by his reaction to the maiden in the tower. Even though he is bewildered by the false priest's interpretation of his dream, he does not suspect him of being other than what he appears to be; yet when confronted with the situation about which the false priest warned him, Bors follows his own sense of what is right rather than the priest's admonitions. And although he has been told, by one ostensibly a priest, that he will refuse the maiden out of pride and therefore commit a grievous sin, he steadfastly, even blindly, holds to his duty to remain chaste and thus does refuse her. At the moment of decision, the safety of his own soul is at issue, and he instinctively does what he must to save it.

The maiden-in-the-tower episode is also real historical narrative, an adventure Bors goes through literally, in waking life. Its meaning and significance are apparent through its relationship to the false priest's explanation which precedes it. The explanation is the distortion of a dream as well as a false model for the ensuing episode. The actual tower incident belies the false priest's explanation and makes clear the deception; it also confirms the rightness of Bors's decision to rescue the maiden in danger of being ravished rather than Lyonel, since the one who tells him his choice was wrong is here revealed to be "l'anemi."

In spite of the deliberate treachery of the false priest's interpretation and instructions, his words do contain a kernel of truth: Bors is warned against holding himself chaste simply for the purpose of winning worldly renown (p. 179, ll. 16–19 [p. 191]). Although Bors is not in immediate danger of this kind of pride, the false priest's words express part of the meaning of the Grail, or at least indicate part of the attitude proper to one engaged in the quest for it. Thus, the entire false priest episode taken as a whole, including the false interpretation of the dream and the maiden in the tower, is for Bors a process of spiritual revelation, for only when it is all over does he understand what has happened to him in dream and adventure. Each part of the episode reverberates onto what goes before and what follows, and each gains new significance by the skillful use of repetition: repeating the same truth in different ways and in different narrative modes—even going so far as to deny the opposite of truth by the words of the false priest (*oppositio*). In this episode, as in that of Priadan le Noir, the interlace of significance and the interlocking of narratives enhance each subdivision, comprehensible and meaningful in itself, in relation to the whole episode.

Finally, the truth of Bors's experience in his quest—and thus the truths expressive of the Grail truths—is repeated in the good abbot's explication of his adventures, visions, and dreams. The episode is a lengthy sermon/explanation of the meanings behind Bors's experience, essentially as has been set forth in the preceding discussion. His explanation is expository, clear, and consistent with exegetical methods. As one of the knights who is worthy of the quest, Bors has had adventures that are significant but which require interpretations, since their meanings are not readily accessible to him. Nonetheless, even though the abbot's explanation contributes to the knight's (and our) understanding of his adventures, it does not in any way subsume the adventures, dreams, and visions it illuminates. The abbot's explanation is not definitive nor any more penetrating than the adventures themselves. It is another repetition, in this case repetition in the expository mode, of truths expressed through other modes of representation. Because of the abrupt changes in levels of narrative—from dream to exposition to real event—that have no narrative or causal connections, it is clear that each encounter is meant to connect with the others as different modes of representing the truth behind events. Repetition of meaning occurs through varied adventures whose relations are analogical, not causal. The episodes are, however, structured by interlace; the same truth may be expressed in a dream, then in real narrative, and finally as part of the priest's or abbot's explication, all the while being interlaced with other events which move among these same levels and throw light on the original episode. Thus, structurally there is not a clear narrative line, and one is forced to read the entire section allegorically. Finally, each representation—imagistic, historical, discursive—emanates from the ultimately ineffable Grail itself.

Confirmation of Bors's worthiness to achieve the Grail quest comes to him from God Himself. As Bors is attempting to protect himself from Lyonel, who tries to kill him for not rescuing him earlier, God orders Bors to put away his sword, sends a lightning bolt that separates and stuns the brothers, and then commands Bors to ride to the sea and enter a waiting ship, which miraculously sails away as soon as he is on board (p. 193, ll. 17–20 [p. 205]).

When daylight comes, Bors discovers Perceval aboard, who, having passed through his own trials, has been awaiting God's will. Thus, at this point two sections, previously separated from each other and each containing the subdivisions or "parts" necessary to provide demonstrations of each knight's response to the Grail adventure, are drawn together to begin a new narrative development.

These parts support and complete each other, as the parts of a Gothic cathedral appear fragmentary and unable to stand alone. As a further analogy to Frankl's description of Gothic architecture, which we have seen includes the concept of Spatial Division, it is important to note that the episodes of the Bors section—as well as those for the other knights—although actually added to each other on the page, function aesthetically as elements of a subdivision. Bors's experience as a quester for the Grail is a whole which has a meaning; this meaning is divided into episodes which demonstrate the effects of this quest upon him. Since the truths embodied in the Grail are ineffable, they can only be partially known by the responses of men to the Grail; and these responses are presented to us as fragmentary, concrete manifestations of it, reflecting the character and moral state of each participating knight as well as the range of his achievement. Thus, we attain only partial and oblique views of that which can never be known entirely but which is the source of meaning in the romance: the Holy Grail itself.

<h2 style="text-align:center">CIRCUMLOCUTIO</h2>

The interrelation of each knight's sections to the others is effected by *circumlocutio*, or *periphrasis*. In the *Queste* the device for signalling new sections, or labyrinthine parts of the "long and winding path," is the dividing statement recounting the end of one section and the beginning of another: *Mes atant lesse ore li contes de . . . et parole de*, or . . . *et retorne a*.[6] Each time such a dividing statement occurs, so frequent in the entire Vulgate Cycle, there is a change of character, setting, and situation. Usually the change is abrupt, the original situation obviously still incomplete. William Ryding sees the dividing statements as related to digression,[7] but digressions turn away for a time from the story at hand whereas the dividing statements introduce interlaced sections which constitute the main narrative lines of the work.[8] The use of these statements to indicate conclusions and beginnings of sections, like the use of *interpretatio* within the sections, contributes substantially to the impression of partiality necessary for the correct understanding of the narrative.

These interruptions function as diagonal members of the romance, much as the ribs express the diagonality of a Gothic cathedral. The statements have two distinct directions, one of which refers backward (*Mes atant lesse ore li contes . . .*) and one forward (*et parole de . . .*), thus emphasizing the interdependence of the parts. This impression is enhanced by having each statement followed, after a break, by phrases indicating the beginning of the next section: *Ore dist li contes que . . .* or *En ceste parti dit li contes que . . .* , which also express the notion of the "part." Because the statement is diagonal, looking in two directions at once, it partakes of both sides yet divides them. Thus, the dividing statements introduce sections which are both interdependent parts of the story of the Grail and yet are members that are deliberately made to appear partial. The dividing statements are, therefore, an admirable structural realization of Geoffrey's dictum; one can, by means of them, circle the subject and "take a long and winding path around what you were going to say briefly."

Evidence that the author(s)[9] of the Vulgate Cycle thought of their work as divided into parts is found in the following authorial statement from the *Lancelot* Proper:

Et furent mande li clerc qui metoient en escript lez proeches des compaignons le roy Artu, si en y avoit .iiij. Si en ot non li uns Arodions de Coloigne, et li secons Tantalides de Vergeaus, et li tiers Thumas de Toulete, et li quars Sapiens de Baudas. Cil quatre metoient en escript tout chou que li compaignon le roy Artu faisoient d'armes, ne ja lor grant feit ne fussent autrement seü; si mistrent en escript lez aventures monseignor Gauvain tout avant, por ce que c'estoit li commenchemens de la queste de Lancelot del Lac. Et puis les granz proeces Hector por ceo qu'il acheva la queste de monseignor Gawain et por chou que de cel conte estoit branche; et puis lez aventures a tous lez .xviij. autres compaignons. Et tout cil autre furent branche de chestui. Et li contes Lancelot fu branche del graal si com il y fu ajoustés.[10] [Citation partially regularized.]

[And they sent for the clerics who put into writing the deeds of prowess performed by King Arthur's companions. There were four of them. The one was named Arodions of Cologne, the second Tantalides of Vergeaus, the third Thumas of Toledo, and the fourth Sapiens of Baudas. These four transcribed all the battles of King Arthur's companions, which otherwise would never have been known about. And they put down the adventures of my Lord Gawain first, since he instigated the quest for Lancelot du Lac. Next came the great deeds of prowess performed by Hector, because it was he who achieved the quest for Gawain and therefore constituted a branch of the Gawain

story. And afterwards were the adventures of eighteen other companions. And all these others were branches of Hector's And the story
of Lancelot was a branch of the Grail, just as it was joined to it.]

It is clear from this statement that the story was conceived of
and presented as parts or "branches" and that the authors
were eager to make clear how the story was arranged into a
hierarchy of ramifications for a proper understanding of it. The
Grail is the source from which the entire cycle emanates, or,
more precisely, the whole of which all the branches are parts.
Our concern here, however, is the effect of all the diagonal
dividing statements between branches within the *Queste* itself.
By means of them the author demarcates the parts by which
the meaning of the Grail is circumlocuted. The way leads
through the quest as structural determinant, to the adventures
as concrete manifestations of the Grail's effects on men, to
each knight's hierarchical ranking as shown by his relative
ability to penetrate spiritual mysteries. At the center of these
circumlocutions stands the Grail itself, made manifest only by
the paths winding towards and away from it.

Quest Structure

Tzvetan Todorov states that "le Graal n'est rien d'autre que
la possibilité d'un récit,"[11] and in fact the narrative it produces
takes the form of much medieval romance, that of the quest.
Paul Zumthor has described the elements of the typical Arthurian quest:

Une situation initiale, généralement provoquée de façon imprévisible,
crée ou révèle l'absence d'un objet ou d'une personne dont l'acquisi-
tion, au cours d'une errance qui suscitera les antagonismes, finit par
être obtenue, pour le plus grand bien du héros et de la communauté à
laquelle il appartient.[12]

Although narrative in the *Queste* is produced by the presence—and then absence—of the Grail, the author's use of the
familiar quest motif by which to organize his narrative departs
in significant ways from the typical pattern Zumthor outlines.
   Although in most romances the goal of the quest is to obtain

an object, find a person, or accomplish a feat, this is not the case in the *Queste*. From the moment the Grail appears at Arthur's court, the quest for it is motivated by the desire to "savoir la verité del Saint Graal" (p. 61, ll. 24–25) [pierce the secret of the Holy Grail (p. 85)]. The mystical nature of this quest, the object of which is to understand the Grail's meaning, separates it from traditional quests, whose primary object is to attain a physical goal.[13] Secondly, a quest normally describes an adventure or series of adventures for which the outcome is not known; this is not true of the *Queste*, since in that work who will achieve the Grail, who will not, and why is for the most part known from the beginning. What is not known is what the Grail is, or means:

Ce sont là deux types différents d'intérêt, et aussi deux types de récit. L'un se déroule sur une ligne horizontale: on veut savoir ce que chaque événement provoque, ce qu'il fait. L'autre represente une série de variations qui s'empilent sur une verticale; ce qu'on cherche sur chaque événement, c'est ce qu'il est. La premier est un récit de contiguïté, le second, de substitutions. Dans notre cas, on sait dès le début que Galaad achèvera victorieusement la quête: le récit de contiguïté est sans intérêt; mais on ne sait pas exactement ce qu'est le Graal et il y a donc la place pour un passionnant récit de substitutions, où l'on arrive, lentement, vers la compréhension de ce qui était posé dès le début.[14]

Finally, this quest is not accomplished "pour le plus grand bien du héros et de la communauté à laquelle il appartient."[15] It could have been if more knights had been successful; if all the questers had been as virtuous as Bors and Perceval, their success would have transformed Arthur's court. But because that court has come to represent worldliness and sin, true achievement of the Grail, such as Galahad's, means that one cannot return to Arthur's court. Galahad's success remains unique, conferring no blessings on that court.[16]

Nonetheless, quest structure is admirably adapted by the author of the *Queste* to his goal: the partial representation in narrative of the meaning of the ineffable Grail. Quest structure allows him to divide possible responses to the Grail into various levels assigned to separate questing knights. We are shown thereby gradations of spiritual worthiness. Each knight is judged by his ability to perceive the truth behind appearances, by his understanding that he is not embarked upon an ordinary quest but upon a spiritual one for which previous standards no longer obtain. This is what determines the character of each knight's quest and his ultimate success or failure. Thus, the dividing statements reflect the divisions the author makes in his narrative, moving from one knight's quest to that of another, all the while circumlocuting the meaning of the Grail as it manifests itself in adventures of different kinds of knights.

Adventure

A *"preudon"* explains to Gawain that "les aventures qui ore avienent sont les senefiances et les demostrances dou Saint Graal, ne li signe dou Saint Graal n'aparront ja a pecheor ne a home envelopé de pechié" (p. 160, l. 33–p. 161, l. 2) [The adventures that you are now to seek concern the nature and manifestations of the Holy Grail; these signs will never appear to sinners or men sunk deep in guilt (p. 174)]. In the *Queste* the success or failure of each knight's quest is determined by his response to potential adventure. But in the world of the *Queste*, "aventure" is not what it had formerly been in, for example, the early parts of the Vulgate Cycle and before that in early verse romance. In Chrétien's romances, "the world of knightly proving is a world of adventure. It not only contains a practically uninterrupted series of adventures; more specifically, it contains nothing but the requisites of adventure. Nothing is found in it which is not either accessory or preparatory to an adventure. It is a world specifically created and designed to give the knight opportunity to prove himself."[17] In adventures of the Prose *Lancelot*, "[knights] are apt to abandon at any time one quest for the sake of another, only to be sidetracked again a moment later. They behave as though this were an accepted mode of living, requiring no apology or explanation, and as though they themselves were involved, not as we would imagine, in a series of unhappy accidents but in an enviable pursuit, to be sought after and enjoyed."[18] What Auerbach and Vinaver refer to is the typical romance adventure, the means by which a knight proves himself and progresses toward perfection. Köhler sees such adventure as the type that occurs by chance or hazard, later to be followed by adventure caused by Providence, and later yet, for example in the *Mort Artu,* by blind Fortune which manifests itself as *mesaventure* or *mescheance.*[19]

In early or pre-*Queste* romance, there are two types of adventure. In the first a knight-errant rides out hoping to find adventures by which to prove himself, so that any adventure he comes upon is welcome and pursued. He may, as Vinaver points out, abandon one adventure for another at any time; the main motivation for his actions is always the hope of demonstrating his prowess. In the second type the knight is on a specific quest, seeking a particular person, place, or thing. Any adventure that presents itself to him during his quest either helps or hinders his progress toward his goal, and he must exercise his judgment as to which of these adventures is to be pursued. He may make mistakes, but he attempts to correct himself and always bears his goal in mind.

What these two types of adventures have in common, and what separates them from adventure in the *Queste,* is that in all cases the knight is active. He encounters a situation and decides whether or not to participate. For the adventures of the Grail, however, these conditions are entirely changed. As the *preudon* counseling Gawain says, these adventures are "les senefiances et les demonstrances dou Saint Graal." In order to have adventures in the *Queste,* a knight must submit himself entirely to God's will and live in a state of preparedness and penance.[20] Passive acceptance of God's will, rather than reliance on one's own prowess, determines success. For a knight to have any adventures in the *Queste* is a sign of his relative worthiness to achieve the final Grail adventure, by which all other adventures are subsumed and to which they lead. Thus, Galahad has more adventures than the narrator relates, while Gawain has none at all. In this context it is clear that adventures do not function as tests of a knight's worthiness in the conventional sense; instead, some knights will have adventures because they are worthy.

However, this does not mean that all is known to us from the beginning. Todorov distinguishes between two kinds of adventure in the *Queste*, narrative and ritual:

avant l'épreuve, Perceval (ou Bohort) n'était pas digne de continuer la recherche du Graal; après elle, s'il réussit, il l'est. Il n'en est pas de même en ce qui concerne Galaad. Dès le début du texte, Galaad est désigné comme le Bon Chevalier, l'invincible, celui qui achèvera les aventures du Graal, image et réincarnation de Jésus-Christ.[21]

However, even if, as in some adventures of Bors and Perceval, the knight does not understand what is occurring, his faith will allow him to take the right course of action. Thus, like Galahad, knights act out of their given characters; they do not become something they were not initially, although it is through adventure that they prove what they are. Those knights like Gawain—and to a lesser extent, Lancelot—who respond to potential adventure as they formerly had, trusting in their own prowess or in love and not perceiving the spiritual nature of the quest, inevitably fail.

The hierarchial ranking of the knights, and thus the outcomes of their respective quests, is made known quite early in the work. Although Galahad's ultimate achievement is known from the first pages, and was even prophesied in the *Lancelot* Proper, it is not long before we learn from Perceval's aunt precisely which knights will succeed and which will fail. The narrative thus operates on two levels: the result of the quest is known from the beginning by God and, through Perceval's aunt, by us; nonetheless, uncertainty hangs over the adventures of Bors, Perceval, and Lancelot as presented, and we fear for the outcome.

Division

The *Queste*'s narrative is presented in the following order, as clearly delineated parts are set off from each other by means of the dividing statements discussed above:

Because the story moves from section to section by means of *circumlocutio* as well as by juxtaposition, the experience of each quester is completed and deepened by that of the others. Moreover, by moving from one knight to another and thus forcing reflection on one knight's adventures in the light of those of another, the author widens the perspective of his story; he is able thereby to express his belief that the meaning of the Grail is greater than the sum of the parts he is able to show. Narrative shifting from knight to knight and back again is an integral facet of the complex interrelationships among adventures. However, in order to illustrate the hierarchical ranking resulting from the response each exemplary knight makes to adventures emanating from the Grail, their experiences on the quest will be examined separately, in the following order:

A. Galahad, the most exalted.

B. Gawain, the most reprobate.

C. Perceval, the closest to Galahad in perfection.

D. Bors, the third elect.

E. Lancelot, the repentant sinner.

A. Galahad.—Galahad's arrival at Arthur's court on the feast of Pentecost announces the beginning of the quest for the

Grail. Even before he appears, mysterious events fraught with significance occur: the *Siege Perilleux* is lettered with words indicating that on that day the master of the seat will arrive (p. 4, ll. 9–11 [p. 33]); the sword in the stone appears in the river with an inscription stating that only the best knight in the world may draw it (p. 5, ll. 23–25 [p. 35]); when the court is seated for dinner, the doors and windows mysteriously close (p. 7, ll. 11–15 [p. 36]). All those present realize the significance of these portents and know that the adventures of the Holy Grail are soon to be brought to an end. Galahad's successful drawing of the sword from the stone and assuming the *Siege Perilleux* are paradigmatic of all his adventures in the *Queste*, including the final achievement of the Grail. He invariably and with no hesitation succeeds in his adventures, partly because he is the *bons chevaliers* for whom these adventures are pre-destined but also because he most perfectly submits his will to God's. Yet Galahad is human; although destined to achieve this quest, he too could fail if he were to sin, as a hermit tells Lancelot (p. 116, ll. 20–25 [p. 134]). By stressing Galahad's free will, the author makes his success more exemplary; he is, like all humans, subject to sin and the errors it causes.

Galahad's adventures are related first in the *Queste*. In the conventional dividing statement before Galahad's initial adventures, the author stresses his importance: "Mes a tant se test ore li contes d'ax toz et parole de Galaad, por ce que comencemenz avoit esté de la Queste" (p. 26, ll. 21–23). [But here the tale leaves them and tells of Galahad, for he it was who had instigated this Quest (p. 53)]. Galahad's adventures always contain spiritual significance. The measure of his perfection is demonstrated by the comparison with other knights who attempt but fail in adventures in which Galahad later succeeds. For example, Baudmagus is wounded nearly to death by a white knight because he attempts to wear the shield that has been reserved for Galahad since it was made by Josephus, the son of Joseph of Arimathea, forty-two years after Christ's death. When Galahad wears it, however, the same white knight who wounded Baudmagus reveals to him the history and significance of the shield, a significance that primarily consists of its being predestined for Galahad. Here is the first link in the *Queste* between sacred history and the present Grail adventures (p. 32, l. 6–p. 35, l. 12 [pp. 58–60]).

Similarly, when the eager Melias, whom Galahad has knighted, pleads with Galahad to allow him to follow the left path, although the warning placed at the crossroads says that he who chooses this path must be second to none, he too is nearly killed (p. 41, l. 2–p. 42, l. 14 [pp. 66–67]). As a monk later explains, the left path is the way of sin, and Melias first committed the sin of pride in believing he could successfully take it. Afterwards, the monk continues, when Melias saw the golden crown the devil set in his way, he immediately fell into the sin of covetousness and thus demonstrated again his spiritual inadequacy. Nonetheless, because Melias made the sign of the cross when the white knight attacked him, God spared his life and sent Galahad to save him (p. 44, l. 32–p. 46. l. 13 [pp. 70–71]). Melias thus serves to demonstrate that ordinary knights cannot achieve the adventures reserved for Galahad because these adventures require spiritual perfection of a kind found only in him. Because all of Galahad's encounters are significant and so, in the context of the *Queste*, qualify as adventures, and because Galahad moves through his adventures with such ease, we need those examples of spiritual failure to apprehend fully the extent of his perfection and achievement. Galahad's adventures have meaning and thus manifest spiritual truths symbolized by the Grail, while those of most other knights do not.

The best measure of the spiritual distance between Galahad and other knights is found in the episode of the Castle of the Maidens. Here Galahad succeeds in single-handedly defeating the seven brothers who hold the castle and in freeing the captive maidens. He does not kill the defeated brothers but instead allows them to flee (p. 46, l. 28–p. 51, l. 16 [pp. 72–76]). However, later Gawain encounters these same seven brothers and, with the help of his companions, kills them (p. 53, ll. 1–16 [p. 78]). Because Gawain does not do penance for his sins, his killing of the seven brothers is not an adventure and has no significance in the quest for the Grail. Yet as a hermit explains to Gawain, Galahad's adventure at the Castle of Maidens has great significance: the seven brothers signify the seven deadly sins, and Galahad's victory over them and rescue of the maidens represents Christ's Harrowing of Hell (p. 55, ll. 1–15 [pp. 79–80]). The hermit goes so far as to explicitly compare Galahad to Christ: "Et tot ausi come il [God] envoia son filz qu'il avoit devant le comencement dou monde, tout einsi envoia il Galaad come esleu chevalier et son esleu serjant" (p. 55, ll. 10–13) [and even as He sent His Son, who was with Him before the begining of the world, even so did He send Galahad, His chosen knight and servant (p. 79)], a comparison that is maintained throughout the *Queste*.

Galahad does of course achieve the final Grail adventures; his entire life is a preparation for them just as the history of the Grail prepares for his coming. His will being at one with God's, in passive acceptance of what God wishes of him, his adventures are synonymous with Grail meaning. His adventures are therefore not so much tests as they are steps in achieving the adventures of Logres leading to the final Grail adventures and the disappearance of the Grail from Logres. By the example of Galahad's achievement of the Grail and saintly death, the author has made manifest in narrative the highest awareness of spiritual truths. Galahad's adventures are a complete paraphrase of the Grail's mysteries.

B. *Gawain.*—At the opposite end of the spectrum from Galahad is Gawain. Steeped in sin, unrepentant and thus unredeemed, he has no conception of what this quest means nor what is required to succeed in it. Although he was the first to vow to seek the Grail (p. 16, ll. 18–25 [p. 44]), he does not understand that *aventure* is now a manifestation of God's mysteries as represented by the Grail and that he is spiritually too blind to perceive them. Because he can think of this quest only in terms of previous knightly pursuits, he is forever complaining about his lack of adventures. For example, to Hector he expresses astonishment that he has met with no adventures even though he has killed many knights: "Car je vos creant loiaument come a mon compaignon que por aler solement, sanz autre besoigne fere, ai je puis ocis plus de dis chevaliers dont li pires voloit assez, ne aventure ne trovai nule" (p. 147, ll. 20–23) [For I swear to you, as you are my companion, that in the course of merely going my way, and no other measures taken, I have slain more than ten knights already, the worst of whom was more than adequate, and still have met with no adventure (p. 162)]. He is, in fact, living a more wicked life than he did before the quest began, for even in the Prose *Lancelot*, the killing of defeated knights was considered unchivalric.

Gawain and Hector, like the other knights, are each accorded a meaningful dream—so meaningful, the author states, that they should be set down lest they be forgotten: "Quant il se furent endormi, si avint a chascun une avision merveilleuse qui ne fet mie a oublier, ainz la doit len bien amentevoir en conte; car assez i a grant senefiance" (p. 149, ll. 11–13) [When they had fallen asleep, each knight had a vision, strange and wonderful; both merit setting down in story lest they be forgotten, for both were rich in meaning (p. 164)]. Unlike the dreams of the other knights, however, Gawain's and Hector's are not veiled moral counsel or revelations of spiritual truth; the two are in fact so lost in sin that the dreams are merely allegorical prefigurations of their ultimate failures in the quest. To Gawain is revealed the end of the quest: of the three elect knights, only Bors will return. His dream also sets forth the ultimate destruction of the Round Table and Arthur's kingdom. And yet Gawain never learns Arthur's fate, as the hermit refuses to interpret this part, lest by doing so he might interfere with the preordained course of events. Hector's dream, besides revealing his own failure in the quest, demonstrates Lancelot's suffering and partial success. Therefore, both dreams illuminate and give new meaning to events far beyond the scope of Gawain's and Hector's actions, while at the same time demonstrating Gawain's and Hector's relative positions in the quest. To the most sinful of knights and the most blind has come the clearest prediction of impending disaster. Yet since Gawain is the least equipped of all the knights to understand, the revelation simply stands as a part of this vast symphony of events, illuminating for the reader all that has gone before it and all that is to follow. For Gawain, however, it is meaningless.

Besides the dreams, Gawain and Hector also have a waking vision in which they are again warned that because of their sinful lives and their refusal to confess and do penance, they will never achieve the adventures of the Grail. Before them pass a hand and forearm draped in red samite, the hand clasping a candle, with a bridle hung over the arm; and a voice speaks to them: "Chevalier plein de povre foi et de male creance, ces troi choses que vos avez orendroit veues vos faillent; et por ce ne poez vos avenir as aventures dou Saint Graal" (p. 151, ll. 4–7) [Knights, weak in faith and erring in belief, these three things you have just looked on are wanting in you; and this is the reason why you cannot attain to the adventures of the Holy Grail (p. 165)]. Hector and Gawain do not understand any of this and determine to find a holy man to interpret for them. This pattern is typical of events in the sections concerning the other knights: a knight has a dream, vision, or adventure, which is later interpreted for him by a priest or hermit. However, in the cases of Bors and Perceval, the knight discovers from the hermits that he has previously acted as the dream instructed, or that the dream is a revelation of further spiritual doctrine which he has proved himself worthy of receiving. Even for Lancelot, the interpretations, although demonstrating the extent of his sinfulness, go on to offer him hope because of his sincere will to change. But Gawain, on his way to find a hermit who will tell him that the vision he saw indicated his lack of charity, abstinance, and truth, kills a knight in a joust, thereby confirming the condemnation in both dream and vision, and also his unworthiness to have any Grail adventures (p. 152, ll. 7–24 [pp. 166–67]). So little does Gawain comprehend the nature of the quest he is embarked on that when he learns that the knight he has killed is Yvain, a worthy knight of the Round Table, he blames it on mischance: "Hé Diex! tant ci a grant mesaventure! Ha! Yvains, tant il me poise de vos!" (p. 153, ll. 31–32) [Oh God! how terrible a misadventure! Ah! Owein, I am sick at heart for you

(p. 168)]. He is clearly unable to relate events to his own sinful behavior. His vision of the world foreshadows that in the *Mort Artu* where God abandons Arthur's world to Fortune and mischance, and thus to destruction.

Further evidence that Gawain's obduracy cannot be penetrated is provided by his encounter with the hermit. After the hermit has delivered a lengthy, detailed interpretation of both dreams and the vision, wherein he makes clear that Gawain and Hector will fail in the quest because of their sinfulness, Gawain can still ask why they do not have adventures anymore (p. 160, ll. 30–32 [p. 174]). The hermit answers him unequivocally: "Les aventures qui ore avienent sont les senefiances et les demostrances dou Saint Graal, ne li signe dou Saint Graal n'aparront ja a pecheor ne a home envelopé de pechié. Dont il ne vos aparront ja; car vos estes trop desloial pecheor" (p. 160, l. 35–p. 161, l. 3) [the adventures that you are now to seek concern the nature and manifestations of the Holy Grail; these signs will never appear to sinners or men sunk deep in guilt, and never therefore to you, for you are most heinous sinners (p. 174)]. Gawain's response to this explicit explanation is not remorseful and repentent, as one would expect; rather, he simply takes it as evidence that it would be senseless for him to continue (p. 161, ll. 7–10 [p. 174]). Hector's response is similar: "se nos vos creions, nos retornerions a Camaalot?" (p. 161, l. 12) [if we took your word for it, we would return to Camelot? (p. 174)]. With no understanding of what they are losing or why, Hector and Gawain quickly and easily give up, and expediently decide to return to Camelot.

Even at the very end of his section, when Gawain is offered a last chance to mend his ways, he refuses for the sake of convenience. The hermit offers to speak to him of his spiritual condition, but Gawain is too eager to catch up with Hector, who has already set off: "se je eusse loisir de parler a vos, je i parlasse volentiers. Mes veez la mon compaignon qui devale le tertre, por quoi il m'en covient aler. Mes bien sachiez que ja si tost n'avré loisir de revenir comme je revendrai; car molt ai grant talent de parler a vos priveement" (p. 161, ll. 23–28) [had I the leisure to talk to you I would do so gladly. But you see my companion making off down the hill, and I must needs go too. But believe me, I shall return as soon as opportunity allows, for I am most anxious to speak with you in private (p. 175)]. He never returns. The feeble promise to do so marks the end of Gawain's significance in the plot. His lack of adventures has served to demonstrate the meaning of the Grail for those who fail to respond and refuse to see.

C. *Perceval.*—Perceval, as one of the three elect knights, represents a level of worthiness immediately below Galahad and almost parallel with Bors. Although Perceval and Bors will succeed in their quests, they are not as perfect as Galahad and must prove themselves by difficult struggle. Thus, the effect of Perceval's experience in the quest is similar to that of Bors, which has been discussed above under *interpretatio*. Similar though the aims of the Bors and Perceval sections are, the adventures recounted in each are widely varied and of divergent significance. Perceval, like the other knights, is the recipient of much spiritual instruction, delivered to him first by a recluse and later by a monk. However, these sermons are very different from those given to Gawain and, as we shall see, to Lancelot. In neither case is Perceval reprimanded for his past life; rather, he receives historical information about the Grail, predictions of the future, and reminders to keep himself chaste. From the recluse, who is also his aunt, Perceval learns who the three Grail knights will be and the history and meaning of the "trois principaus tables ou monde" (p. 74, l. 21 [p. 97]): the Table of the Last Supper, the Table of the Grail established by Joseph of Arimathea, and the Round Table. Thus, Perceval is told things he wants and needs to know but also is informed of matters bearing on the other knights.

The major theme of the recluse's sermon to Perceval is *luxure*. She uses Lancelot's long love for Guinevere as an example of *luxure*, a sin that could also keep Perceval from achieving the Grail. She congratulates him for preserving his virginity thus far and makes clear that it is his chastity that has earned him a place among the Grail knights. But she warns him that should he lose it, he will lose his place among them, as Lancelot already has (p. 80. ll. 1–17 [p. 102]). Chastity is a sign of worthiness in the *Queste*, and the three elect knights represent various degrees of it: Galahad, never tempted, is first; Perceval, sorely to be tempted but remaining a virgin, is second; and Bors, sinning once but against his will and having done penance, is third.

Perceval's temptation—and most important test—occurs when the devil assumes the shape of a beautiful woman. Coming as it does after the recluse's implicit and explicit reflections on Lancelot's sinful life, the test casts further light on the characters of the two knights. When Perceval finds himself alone on the barren island filled with wild animals, he first proves himself by putting his trust in God: "Si se fie plus en s'aide et en son secors qu'il ne fet en s'espee, car ce voit il bien que par proesce de chevalerie terriane n'en porroit il eschaper, se Nostre Sires n'i metoit conseil" (p. 93, ll. 27–30) [He trusted more in His help and succour than in his sword, for he saw most plainly that no prowess achieved with this world's arms would suffice to save him unless Our Lord came to his aid (p. 114)]. This is contrary to the practice of Lancelot, who, regardless of his good intentions, is seldom able to trust completely in God and to give up reliance on his own prowess. [22]

Perceval's real triumph lies in his escaping—albeit just in the nick of time—from the bed of the devil disguised as a beautiful maiden bent on his destruction. Like Bors in a similar situation, Perceval makes the sign of the cross, and the maiden-devil flees in smoke and shrieking. It might be argued that since Perceval makes the sign of the cross almost automatically and is certainly not consciously trying to escape, his victory can hardly be to his credit and therefore should not be compared with Lancelot's overcoming his long-time love for Guinevere. Nonetheless, Perceval's faith is such—"car il estoit un des chevaliers dou monde qui plus parfetement creoit en Nostre Seignor" (p. 95, ll. 13–14) [for he stood out among all the knights of his time for his perfect faith in Our Lord (p. 115)]—that for this, his first fall, God intervenes to let Perceval's eyes fall on the cross upon his sword hilt, which brings him back to himself. Unlike Lancelot, Perceval did not consciously and consistently pursue a sinful love. As the *preudon* on the white ship says, "Ha! Perceval . . . toz jorz seras tu nices!" (p. 112, ll. 25–26) [Ah, Perceval, . . . you will ever be simple (p. 131)]. Perceval is simple indeed—both in the sense of being uncomplicated and of being a simpleton—but it is the very simplicity of his faith and the lack of forethought through which he nearly falls that distinguish him from Lancelot, who until the time of the *Queste* is "li mieldres chevaliers del monde" (p. 5, l. 27) [the best knight of the world (p. 35)], and who, unlike Perceval, has always remained "of the world."

Perceval has adventures, and he proves himself by means of them. His faith in God and his sincere penance for sin rank him among the elect knights, those worthy to see unveiled the secrets of the Grail. He is not Galahad: his victory is not a forgone conclusion; but his adventures, in which faith allows him to triumph, define him as chosen by God.

D. Bors.—As one of the elect knights, Bors, like Galahad and Perceval, succeeds in his adventures. However, consonant with the *Queste* author's intention to circumlocute the meaning of the Grail by demonstrating various levels of response to its presence, Bors's adventures distinguish him from the other two Grail knights. He does achieve the Grail, but he is third of the elect knights and is, after all, the only one of them to return to Camelot when the quest is over. Since Bors's adventures have been discussed in detail above under *interpretatio* as an example of the complex interrelationship of parts within each narrative section, it is necessary here to note only his relationship to the other questing knights.

Bors shows a kind and level of response to the quest different from what we have seen heretofore; even among knights at nearly the same spiritual level, the author has nuanced their adventures and reactions so that after the Bors section we feel as though we know man's principal spiritual conditions. This is because Bors is implicitly contrasted not only to Gawain but to the other knights as well. Unlike Lancelot, he does not feel alien in a changed world; as Pauphilet states, "Bohort comprend comme il faut la vie terrestre et sa signification religieuse."[23] And Pauphilet continues, "Il discerne clairement le parti de Dieu au milieu des visions ambiguës et des fantasmagories trompeuses. Les doutes proposés à son esprit, les tentations offertes à sa chair, il les repousse également."[24] This is clear in the false priest episode, where Bors does not actually see through the deceptive appearances but still eschews fallacious counsel. He holds steadfastly to what he knows is right, guarding the salvation of his soul by his very goodness.

Besides contrasting markedly with Gawain and demonstrating the spiritual vision that Lancelot unsuccessfully struggles to attain, Bors's experience illuminates the adventures of the two other successful knights. He is not so nearly perfect in spirituality as Galahad. No one can be, since Galahad represents a type of Christ who remains totally untainted by the world even if, like Christ, he can be tempted. Thus, there is a clear hierarchical distinction between Bors's and Galahad's levels of worthiness. Furthermore, the sections devoted to Bors and Perceval throw each of them into relief and reveal different kinds of spiritual response. Bors triumphs in his quest by means of patience and humility; as Pauphilet points out: "C'est par la patience, nous dirions l'acceptation de la souffrance, qu'il triomphe des ennemis du Christ; c'est par l'humilité, par la prière agenouillée, qu'il répond aux fureurs d'un ennemi."[25] As we have seen earlier, patience and humility are not Perceval's strengths; he is neither reflective nor prudent, and he is childlike in his lack of suspicion or guile. Unlike Bors, who rejects the temptation of the devil, "à la première attaque de l'Ennemi [Perceval] se laisse prendre comme un enfant."[26] Nonetheless, he possesses perfect faith and innocence and thus "Perceval verra les grands mystères; il est le type de ceux qui se justifient par la foi, comme Bohort l'est de ceux qui se justifient par les œuvres."[27] And here lies the real difference between them: faith and works. Although both will be admitted to the secrets of the Grail, Perceval attains his worthiness to do so by means of perfect faith and innocence; Bors attains it by conscientious effort, persistance, and prudent actions.

E. *Lancelot.*—On the ladder of worthy knights, Lancelot is immediately above Gawain; it has been mentioned that he is, before the Grail quest begins, "li mieldres chevaliers del monde" (p. 5, l. 27 [p. 35], whose partial success in the quest for the Grail is far more complex than the failure experienced by Gawain. Lancelot's adventures are divided into three stages: his realization of his past sinful life and its consequences; his attempt to purify and transform himself through confession and penance, through hardships and the aid of hermits and other religious men and women; and his partial vision of the Grail secrets. Interspersed throughout these separate sections on various levels are the themes of blindness and the inadequacy of earthly prowess in his quest, as well as the lesson of the Parable of the Talents (Q. p. 63, l. 13–p. 64, l. 13 [p. 87]; Matthew 25: 14–30). Lancelot's progressive understanding serves as a measure of his spiritual growth.

Lancelot's initial moral blindness and lack of understanding are made clear by his complete inability to respond to the presence of the sick knight and the Holy Grail. Although he sees and hears everything that takes place, he can neither move nor speak (p. 59, ll. 22–27 [p. 83]). Lancelot's impotence stems from his lack of virtue, or moral fortitude. After hearing a voice accuse him of being harder than stone, more bitter than wood, and more barren than a fig tree, Lancelot himself comes to realize that his blindness comes from his past sinful life, particularly his *luxure* (p. 62, ll. 1–7 [pp. 85–86]).

Nonetheless, Lancelot is far from achieving full insight into his spiritual state and has a long way to go before becoming worthy of even his partial experience of the Holy Grail, as his attitude the morning after his vision demonstrates. He is disconsolate, "Car la ou il cuidoit joie trover et toutes honors terrianes a il failli, ce est as aventures dou Saint Graal; et ce est une chose qui mout le desconforte"(p. 62, ll. 16–19) [For there where he had thought to find all joy and honour and worldly acclaim, in the adventures of the Holy Grail, he had reaped only failure and its bitter gall (p. 86)]. At this point Lancelot regrets his *luxure* primarily because it has cost him "honors terrianes"; he does not yet understand that "honors terrianes" are not pertinent to his quest.

After this adventure Lancelot meets a hermit and thus begins his long, intense education in the spiritual life. His sins and mistakes are clearly pointed out to him by various hermits and holy men and women, along with vivid descriptions of the consequences if he continues in the ways of the world. But since Lancelot, unlike Gawain, does want to reform his ways, he is also assured of God's forgiveness if he is steadfast in his purpose. It is at this point that Lancelot confesses for the first time in the entire cycle his love for Guinevere, at the same time ascribing all his successes and virtues to his love for her (p. 66, ll. 13–16 [p. 89]). Nonetheless, he proves himself more worthy than Gawain by his readiness to accept a penance—the wearing of the hair shirt—and holy instruction; yet because of his years of sinful living, the way for him will be hard.

Lancelot's second stage consists of a series of humiliations, chastenings, and instructions and explanations leading finally to a higher level of understanding and partial purification. Yet, as Pauphilet says, Lancelot is not raised to perfection; his long life of sin causes him to fall into error and failure: "Lancelot est devenu pieux, austère et bon, mais il ne comprend pas toujours le langage mystique que parle le monde sensible: il lui arrive de se tromper, et il faut sans cesse que des religioux l'éclairent et le guident."[28] Unlike Bors, with his firm faith and determination, and Perceval, with his simple and perfect faith, Lancelot does not simply do what is right; he does not move easily among things that are not what they seem; he lacks, as Pauphilet rightly points out, "la confiance totale en Dieu, l'oubli de la raison terrestre, le sens du miracle."[29] And because Lancelot's adventures, like all the others, incorporate various modes—dreams, visions, and present narrative history—he is often bewildered, constantly dependent on religious people for explanations and help.

A hermit directly relates Lancelot's blindness to *luxure*; after the latter enumerates all the virtues that inhered in Lancelot prior to his sin—chastity being chief among them—he explains how Lancelot was set on a new path, "la voie de luxure" (p. 125, l. 35–p. 126, l. 1) [the path of lust (p. 143)]. From the time the devil set Lancelot's mind on Guinevere, the knight has been blinded: "Des lors te toli li anemis la veue (p. 126, ll. 2–3) [From that time on the enemy robbed you of your sight (p. 143)]. Nonetheless, because God had given Lancelot so many talents, there were some left over, hence, his fame and renown. This is contrary to Lancelot's earlier opinion that all his feats of prowess were due to his love for Guinevere (p. 66, ll. 8–16 [p. 89]). From the hermit he learns that his achievements were possible *in spite of* his love for Guinevere (p. 126, ll. 23–29 [p. 143]). Thus, Lancelot's education progresses, and after further injunctions by the hermit, he renounces his former life, aware of where it has led him (p. 128, ll. 27–30 [p. 145]); yet because of that past, his view of what is required in his new life remains unclear.

In spite of the careful spiritual education Lancelot receives from the religious men he encounters and the apparent progress in purification of his soul, he fails the test of the tournament between the white and the black knights—a situation whose moral implications are by now readily apparent to any reader of the *Queste*[30]—in which he chooses to help the black knights (p. 140, l. 5–p. 142, l. 13 [pp. 155–57]). This is nothing new for Lancelot, who has always chosen to help the losing side, and in the pre-*Queste* world such behavior would have been magnanimous. Here, then, is clear evidence of Lancelot's inability to deal with a world whose rules have changed and where events are not just themselves but represent moral truths as well. Although armed with the best of intentions, once Lancelot is on his own in the figural world of the *Queste* and not under the direct tutelage of a hermit, he falls quickly into error as a result of his long blindness to the spiritual world.

Lancelot does, however, come close to understanding what is required in this quest when circumstances force him to rely on God. Faced with the River Marcoise to ford, he puts his faith in God rather than trusting in his own prowess; he accepts even the death of his horse as God's will. Lancelot is trapped on all sides: the river is in front of him, huge cliffs rise on either side, and a deep forest lies behind. He perceives that he can only wait passively upon God's will, as Galahad, Bors and Perceval always do. Lancelot knows himself to be powerless: "Si ne set tant esgarder de nule part de ces trois parties qu'il i voie sauveté terriane" (p. 146, ll. 20–21) [With whatever attention he considered these obstacles, he could see no salvation here below (p.161)]. Through suffering and humiliation, Lancelot has been led to an understanding heretofore unknown to him and has attained at least a certain lucidity.

Because of his sincere intent and good will, Lancelot receives many rewards. He is told by a hermit that he will come finally to the castle of the Grail and will have Galahad's company (p. 249, ll. 6–23 [p. 256]). He receives the grace of the Holy Spirit while drifting in the boat (p. 250, l. 1 [p. 257]), he does have the joy of Galahad's company for six months (p. 251, l. 22 [p. 258]), and he experiences a partial revelation of the secrets of the Grail (p. 255, ll. 14–25 [p. 262]).

Nonetheless, the reward is partial, and Lancelot's ultimate failure to participate fully in the Grail ceremony is directly related to his flaws. When God tells him to enter the Castle of Corbenic, he draws his sword to fight his way past the lions guarding the gate. This is evidence anew of trust in his own prowess rather than in God. The reprimand is swift and harsh: "Ha! hons de povre foi et de mauvese creance, por quoi te fies tu plus en ta main que en ton Criator?" (p. 253, ll. 22–24) [O man of little faith and most infirm belief, why placest thou greater trust in thine own arm than in thy Maker? (p. 260)]. Similarly, although warned not to enter the room where the Grail ceremony is taking place, Lancelot, in a gesture of good will, forgets himself and steps forward to help the priest for whom the body of Christ appears too heavy (p. 255, l. 26–p. 256, l. 3 [p. 262]). Thus, he constantly backslides into earthly error; his past sins prevent him, in spite of sincere intentions, from seeing the spiritual truth behind earthly events.

Yet in Lancelot's punishment for lack of spiritual insight lies also his reward. While he is unconscious for twenty-four days, God vouchsafes him spiritual visions of such glory that when he wakens he wishes to have remained in that state forever. And it is after this experience that Lancelot finally understands his own spiritual blindness and what it has cost him (p. 258, ll. 10–13 [p. 264]). However, for Lancelot, it is then too late; he is told by those of the castle, "vostre queste est achevee; por noient vos travailleroiz plus por quierre le Saint Graal; car bien sachiez que vos n'en verroiz plus que veu en avez" (p. 259, ll. 2–4)[31] [your quest is ended; there is no use your striving any longer to seek the Holy Grail; for you should know that you will not see more of it than you have seen (p. 265)]. Lancelot has achieved the highest adventure of the Grail available to him because he has gone as far as possible to overcome the effect of sin on his spiritual condition.[32] *Circumlocutio*, with the diagonal views it provides onto other knights, defines Lancelot's spiritual state; and the implicit comparisons between Lancelot and the elect knights, and also between Lancelot and the irredeemable knights Gawain and Hector, throw his position into relief. When Lancelot's quest is over, his relation to the entire story and to the meaning of the Grail quest has been so subtly delineated by purely structural means—concomitants of diagonality like oblique views and juxtaposed divisions inviting comparisons—that the conclusion to his quest comes to us with the force of inevitability.

For the same reasons we are not surprised at the end of this section by the fates of Hector and Gawain. Hector fulfills the prediction of his own dream by riding up to the Castle at Corbenic on a powerful horse—which the hermit had previously interpreted as Pride—and demanding entry. As he had dreamed, Hector is refused entry to the Grail feast by King Pelles, speaking in tones usually reserved to God: "Sire chevaliers, vo n'i entrerez; ja nus qui si haut soit montez come vos estes n'i entrera, tant com li Sainz Graax i soit. Mes alez vos en vostre païs, car certes vos n'estes pas des compaignons de la Queste, ainz estes de çax qui ont lessié le servise Jhesucrist et se sont mis ou servise a l'anemi"[33] (p. 260, ll. 6–11) [Sir Knight, you shall not enter; no man so proudly mounted as yourself shall enter here so long as the Holy Grail is within. Go back to your own country; for you are surely no companion of the Quest, but rather one of those who have quit the service of Jesus Christ to become the liegeman of the enemy (p. 266)]. Although Hector has literally "found" the Grail, he has in no way followed the right path spiritually, and so his quest must end in failure and shame.

Gawain's final appearance—appropriately *in absentia*—is also typical of what we have come to expect of him and is final demonstration of his imperviousness to all spiritual instruction. His quest has been constantly characterized by the search for adventures, which he never ceased interpreting in the old way to include jousting and prowess, and so, tragically, he moved further and further away from the possiblity of achieving the quest. When Lancelot finds the tomb of good King Bademagu with the inscription declaring that Gawain slew him, we have explicit testimony to the utter failure of Arthur's renowned nephew (p. 261, ll. 28–32 [p. 268]). He who so eagerly began the quest never understood what he sought. Yet because of the continually interweaving sections describing the variety of experiences and responses of those engaged on the quest, we as readers do know both what he lost and how he lost it.

When the tests end, all the knights except the elect have dropped away. Only the final Grail ceremonies remain and the final revelations to those who have proved worthy. Adventure as manifestation of the Grail's effects on men has allowed the *Queste*'s author to demonstrate and define worthiness for us. However, just as *circumlocutio* permits us to comprehend the knight's characters through their adventures, it also allows us to approach the Grail's meaning through these characters.

Vinaver has written of medieval romance that "we are in an age when character has no existence outside destiny, and destiny means the convergence of simultaneously developed themes, now separated, now coming together, varied, yet synchronized, so that every movement of this carefully planned design remains charged with echoes of the past and premonitions of the future."[34] It is the interweaving and juxtaposition of the knightly adventures by means of *circumlocutio* that define character in the *Queste*; and far from being an end in itself, character is a narrative element used by the author to demonstrate both various ways of seeking the Grail and various levels of response to it.

These levels are types of the possible responses to the Grail; thus, the delineation of character in the *Queste* conforms to medieval instruction and practice on the subject,[35] as expressed by Matthew of Vendôme:

> Further, let the understanding of the student commit to trusty memory the fact that he must perceive the general principles behind the specific names in the above descriptions [of the Pope, Caesar, etc.], lest he presume to a private understanding that differs from the intention of the author . . . . Hence the attributes assigned to the Pope, or Caesar, or the rest, must be understood in such a way that the particular name does not outweigh the relevance of these attributes to other persons of the same condition, age, dignity, office or sex. The particular designation should be taken to stand for a general designation according to the nature of the subject and not according to the subject used to exemplify that nature.[36]

In the *Queste* adventure is the means whereby we are led to know the knight's characters and to understand their "general designations." Gawain's response to any potential Grail adventure defines him as an example of the incorrigible sinner. And so it is with the other knights: each responds in accordance with his hierarchical ranking. We only come to know this ranking, however, through each knight's revealing of his character in the face of Grail adventures. The interpenetration of knightly adventures, the careful orchestration of the narrative—each section "charged with echoes of the past and premonitions of the future," each knight's adventures reflecting on the others'—gives the story its depth and suggestions of meaning beyond what can be totally known.

The Mysteries of the Grail.—The last section of the *Queste* contains the achievement of the Grail by Galahad. This is the goal to which all that has gone before has been subordinated and whose meaning the structure of the work adumbrates. Clearly, Geoffrey's dictum for *circumlocutio* has been heeded; the literal path of quests has led to the Grail ceremony at Sarras. All the sections of the *Queste*, "hints" of what is necessary for the achievement of the Grail, find their final meaning in this section, and its effect is to cast our mind's eye backward with greater enlightenment and understanding of significances only dimly perceived previously. The process of learning has been incremental, for as we have seen, each section of the *Queste*, each portion of a given knight's adventures, has been illuminated by those that have come before; and each portion itself provides perspective on those that follow. Through *circumlocutio* the author has presented the effects of the Grail in parts; when the *Queste* is over, our knowledge of the Grail itself remains partial. We know no more than what Galahad can express: "car ore voi ge tot apertement ce que langue ne porroit descrire ne cuer penser" (p. 278, ll. 4–5) [for now I see revealed what tongue could not relate nor heart conceive (p. 283)]. If Galahad, the one to see the Grail secrets clearly and openly, cannot express what he has seen and is then transported to the celestial plane where human limitations no longer obtain, we must be content with the partial views which the author, through the careful structuring of narrative sections, provides us. Like the oblique, diagonal vistas presented by a Gothic cathedral, the aspects of the Grail unveiled by the author through the unwinding of his narrative leave us with partial knowledge of the ultimately ineffable.

DIGRESSIO

Thus far we have seen how the author of the *Queste* presents partial insight into the meaning of the Grail, revealing its truths through the *synecdochic* mode in two ways: the narrative divisions produced by *interpretatio*, repeating meanings in varied forms as illustrated by the discussion of the Bors section; and the diagonal views resulting from *circumlocutio*, the "long and winding path" through the alternating quests and adventures of exemplary knights, with the *interpretationes* this path also produces. The partial meaning of the Grail is represented by a third technique of amplification: *digressio*. The *Queste* author turns aside from the Arthurian Grail quest to introduce historical material remote from it but which completes the quest's meaning on the level of sacred history, usually of an apocryphal kind. Such digressions expand the significance of the Arthurian moment to partake of and fulfill the past. Presented as incomplete segments in the Grail history, each digression is fragmentary and depends on other digressions as well as present events to complete its meaning in relation to the Grail.

The historical manifestations of the Grail and its mysteries define partially the vessel by both analogical and figural means. Present events are explained by the past as well as completing that past; the interlacing of past events related to the Grail with the adventures of the quest for, and the final achieving of, the Grail itself produces an interpenetration of past and present that transcends time and, with it, cause and effect as they are usually understood. We approach the whole —the meaning of the Grail—here too by hints and perceptions that are meaningful but not causal and not explicit; rather, they are the working out of the aims of Providence on a background of human inequity stemming from the Fall of Adam and Eve. These historical manifestations are presented in eight separate narrative blocks, at first spaced far apart in the work and then building up with increasing frequency until they culminate in the Tree of Life episode, where historical digression occupies an entire section. With this section all that is necessary to know has been told, and the preparation for the final Grail scene is complete.[37]

(I) The first digression occurs after Galahad's inquiry at the very beginning of his adventures regarding the shield given to him by the White Knight (p. 31, l. 31–p. 32. l. 2 [p. 58]). The knight relates to Galahad the story of Joseph of Arimathea, who was the first to possess the Grail; the conversion of Evalach/Mordrain and Nascien; Joseph's son Josephus's captivity in Britain and Mordrain's rescue of him; and the conversion of Britain. The shield by which Josephus converted his rescuer is received by Mordrain from Josephus as a remembrance of him upon the latter's death; moreover, Josephus stipulates that Galahad, the last of Nascien's line, shall receive it five days after he is made a knight. The shield is to be placed where Nascien wishes his body to be laid, to ensure that Galahad will find it (p. 32, l. 6–p. 35, l. 12 [pp. 58–60]). This narration reveals to Galahad part of his lineage and why he is the rightful owner of the shield; it also explains the dreadful reputation the sword has gained: those who have attempted to possess it have been punished by God because they were not entitled to it. Obviously, the interpretation given here does not explain anything in causal terms; placing the sword where Nascien's body lies does in no way guarantee Galahad's finding it, much less precisely five days from his knighting. Yet in terms of the typological significance of the *Queste*, the explanation is entirely satisfying; past events are recounted only to prefigure the achieving of the Grail, and Galahad, as the one who will achieve it, is connected to the past.

(II) The next historical digression on the Grail occurs in the context of Perceval's instructions by his aunt, specifically in answer to his question about the mysterious knight Galahad. The answer relates the history of the three tables: the Table of the Last Supper, the Table of the Holy Grail and Joseph of Arimathea, and the Round Table. The tables are drawn together in a figural relationship that defines Galahad as a type of both Christ and Josephus, Joseph's son: "Vos savez bien que Jhesucriz fu entre ses apostres pastres et mestres a la table de la Ceinne; aprés fu senefiee par Joseph la Table del Saint Graal, et la Table Reonde par cest chevalier" (p. 78, ll. 7–10) [You are not ignorant that Jesus Christ presided as shepherd and master among His apostles at the table of the Last Supper. Later the Table of the Holy Grail acquired this meaning through Josephus, and the Round Table through this knight (p. 100)]. The meaning of the Grail itself is further unveiled by the significances attached to it through the three tables; by means of the analogy among them, Galahad's achievement of the Grail comes to be prefigured by Christ's Passion, and thus all of Christian history is drawn into the network of events related to the Grail ceremony at Sarras, during which Galahad dies and passes to heaven. What we learn of the Grail history here is layered upon what was imparted in the first digression and both broadens our knowledge of the Grail's fate in the time of Joseph and extends its import back to the time of Christ.

(III) The story of the Maimed King is told to Perceval by a priest (p. 83, l. 21–p. 87, l. 2 [pp. 105–8]). Here the story of Mordrain's rescue of Josephus from prison is retold, with the additional information that Josephus and his followers, although given no food or water, were sustained by the Holy Grail. [38] The narrative adds—and this is the significant feature of the retelling—the episode of King Mordrain's being blinded and wounded by God for his presumptuous attempt to come closer to the Holy Grail. The story prepares for Galahad's later healing of Mordrain and connects it with the history of the Grail; in answer to Mordrain's prayer, God allows him to survive from the time of Joseph of Arimathea to that of the achieving of the Grail. The fact of a character surviving for over four hundred years in itself mirrors the subjection of historical time and causality to transcendent meaning.

The interpenetration of the past with the actual adventures of the Grail is enhanced by analogy. Mordrain's longing to see the Grail along with his forgetfulness of God's proscription, prefigures Lancelot's Grail experience; like Lancelot in his twenty-four-day trance, Mordrain is covered by a cloud "qui li toli la veue des elz et le pooir dou cors" (p. 85, ll. 16–17) [which robbed him of his sight and strength (p. 106)]. And they both describe what they have experienced of the Grail in the same terms: "langue mortiex nel porroit dire ne cuers terriens penser" (p. 85, ll. 13–14) [the tongue of man could not relate nor human heart conceive (p. 106)]. Thus, Lancelot becomes connected with the Grail history, and Mordrain—besides his healing—with its present. The last analogy here is explicit; the priest likens Simeon's waiting for the infant Christ with Mordrain's waiting for Galahad: "Et ausi come cil atendoit o grant desirrier Jhesuchrist le filz Dieu, le haut Prophete, le souverain Pastre, ausi atent ore cist rois la venue de Galaad, le Bon Chevalier, le parfet" (p. 86, ll. 29–32) [And even as Simeon thirsted after Jesus Christ, the Son of God, the most high Prophet and the one true Shepherd, even so this king now waits for the coming of Galahad, the good and perfect knight (pp. 107–8)]. Galahad's identification as a type of Christ further enhances the significance of that which he is destined to achieve.

(IV) The next historical manifestation of the Grail secrets is granted to Lancelot (p. 134, l. 13–p. 138, l. 8 [pp. 151–54]), who by the time he receives it, has attained greater understanding. He requires explanation of a dream, and the hermit interprets by means of a dream of Mordrain's. Both dreams reveal Galahad's lineage and thus include Lancelot. In Mordrain's dream nine rivers correspond to the seven kings and two knights in Lancelot's dream. The hermit interprets by means of the history of Joseph of Arimathea—already familiar to us—and continues down through the line, describing the spiritual perfection of each king. In both dreams Galahad is singled out as the elect of God, but only in Lancelot's dream is Lancelot's own sin documented. However, the two dreams cause history to come together in a singular way, in that Mordrain dreams of a lineage that is to follow while Lancelot dreams of the same lineage after it is already established. Yet because of the hermit's use of Mordrain's dream to interpret Lancelot's, as narrative they occur at one and the same time. It is the destined achievement by Galahad of the Grail, whose significance is not bound by time, that effects the simultaneity of events that are separated only literally in time.

(V–VII) The next three historical manifestations of the Grail are revealed to Bors, Perceval, and Galahad by Perceval's sister while they are on the Ship of Solomon. Her immediate purpose is to explain the inscriptions found on objects in the ship; but the explanations also serve to connect past and present in a complex of significant events emanating from the Grail mysteries. The first inscription explained is found on that part of the miraculous sword emerging from the scabbard:

JA NUS NE SOIT TANT HARDIZ QUI DOU FUERRE ME TRAIE, SE IL NE DOIT MIELZ FERE QUE AUTRE ET PLUS HARDIEMENT. ET QUI AUTREMENT ME

TRERA, BIEN SACHE IL QU'IL N'EN FAUDRA JA A ESTRE MORZ OU ME-
HAIGNIEZ. ET CESTE CHOSE A JA ESTÉ ESPROVEE AUCUNE FOIZ. (p. 203, ll.
27–31)

[LET NONE PRESUME TO DRAW ME FROM THE SCABBARD, UNLESS HE CAN
OUTDO AND OUTDARE EVERY OTHER. HE WHO IN ANY OTHER CIRCUM-
STANCE UNSHEATHES ME SHOULD KNOW HE IS FOREDOOMED TO INJURY
OR DEATH. THE TRUTH OF THIS REQUIRES NO FURTHER PROVING. (p.
215)].

Perceval's sister explains part of the mystery of the sword by
telling the story of the battle between King Lambar, the father
of the Maimed King, and King Varlan. The latter, in extremity
and not heeding the warning on the sword, drew it to kill King
Lambar and with this first blow ever struck by the sword in
Logres, caused the land to be laid waste (p. 204, ll. 26–28 [p.
216]). When he attempts to possess the scabbard as well, King
Varlan himself is struck down dead. Unspecified in time, the
story takes place somewhere in the past and integrates the
Waste Land theme with that of the adventures of the Grail. It
furthers the theme of Galahad as elect knight, for the whole
ruin of Logres is due to the presumption of those who attempt
adventures reserved to Galahad.

The inscription on the other side of the blade has two parts,
with a separate historical foundation for each. The first part
reads:

CIL QUI PLUS ME PRISERA PLUS I TROVERA A BLASMER AU GRANT BESOIGN
QUE IL NEL PORROIT CUIDIER. (p. 206, ll. 15–16)

[HE THAT SHALL PRIZE ME MOST SHALL FIND ME WORTHIER OF REPROACH
IN TIME OF NEED THAN HE COULD DREAM. (p. 217)]

To explain this, Perceval's sister relates an adventure of
Nascien's. He was on the Ship of Solomon for eight days,
resisting the temptation to draw the sword because of the
warning that he who prized it most would find most to reproach it for in his hour of need. However, upon landing and
meeting a "jaiant," he seized the sword to defend himself, but
it broke in half, fulfilling the warning. Further punishment

was given to Nascien when he met and entered Mordrain's ship, only to be wounded in the shoulder by a flying sword. God explained: "Ce est por le forfet que tu feis de l'espee que tu tresis: car tu n'i devoies pas adeser, car tu n'en estoies pas dignes" (p. 208, ll. 30–32) [This is for the wrong thou didst in drawing the sword: thou shouldst not have touched it, for thou wert unworthy (p. 220)]. Thus, the theme of Galahad's predestination is adumbrated: all those, however worthy— and Nascien is represented as being without spiritual flaws— who attempt adventures meant for Galahad are punished. This digression serves both to heighten the identification of Galahad with the Grail adventure and to link present and past history by means of objects.

The rest of the inscription on the sword reads:

ET A CELUI A QUI JE DEVROIE ESTRE PLUS DEBONERE SERAI JE PLUS FELONESSE. ET CE N'AVENDRA FORS UNE FOIZ, CAR EINSI LE COVIENT ESTRE A FORCE. (p. 206, ll. 16–19)

[AND TO HIM TO WHOM I SHOULD BE KINDEST I SHALL SHOW MYSELF MOST CRUEL. THIS WILL OCCUR BUT ONCE, FOR SO IT IS ORDAINED. (p. 217)]

The explanation given by Perceval's sister accounts for the Maimed King. King Parlan, known widely for his Christian virtue, presumptiously drew the miraculous sword partly out of its scabbard and for this action was wounded in the thighs by a flying lance. He is to remain maimed until Galahad comes to him. The warning that the sword would be most cruel to whom it should be most kind was thus fulfilled, "car il ert li mieldres chevaliers et li plus preudons qui alors fust" (p. 210, ll. 3–4) [for there was no better man or knight . . . in his day (p. 221)]. Besides providing necessary explanations for the existence of the Maimed King, this digression continues the theme of adventures to be undertaken only by Galahad and the presumption of those who consider themselves worthy of such feats. Historical interpenetration is effected here in two ways: historical epochs are linked by means of an object, the sword; and history is also dissolved, by means of the Maimed King's remaining alive and waiting for Galahad to heal him.

The ultimate healing of the Maimed King during the Grail ceremony at Corbenic merges these themes in the complex of significances surrounding the Grail.

(VIII) Three of the narratives discussed above begin with a close varient of the phrase, "Il avint jadis, bien a quarante ans après la Passion Jhesucrist" (p. 32, ll. 6–7; p. 134. l. 13; p. 206, ll. 32–33 [p. 58; p. 151; p. 218]). It locates those episodes in time shortly after the Passion. The temporal interpenetration of the past with the present shows the Grail to contain meanings related to the Passion. In the Legend of the Tree of Life section, however, these meanings are extended back to the beginning of sacred history. The story of Adam and Eve, typologically a traditional prefiguration of Christ's mission, now becomes a part of the story of the Grail (p. 210, l. 29–p. 226, l. 7 [pp. 222–35]).

The collapse of history into the meaning of the Grail in this section is effected by means of lineage, physical objects, and analogical references. The Miraculous Ship, on board which Perceval's sister explains the inscription, was built by Solomon in an effort to make Galahad know Solomon's foreknowledge of the coming of Galahad, the last of Solomon's lineage. Through the voice of God, we learn that Galahad descends not only from Nascien but that his lineage begins, through Solomon, with King David and thus even passes obliquely through the Virgin Mary. Hence, Galahad's general typological identification with Christ throughout the *Queste* is paralleled by an actual relationship which, though never stated explicitly, is implied in his descent from the Virgin.

The ship itself is also a means of dissolving history, since it comes from the time of Solomon. The sword containing the inscriptions described above was King David's; the hilt and pommel of the sword were made by Solomon, and the bed and coverlets were placed on the ship by Solomon's wife. Most significant, however, are the three beams of wood attached to the bed. They are made of wood from the Tree of Life in the Garden of Eden, a twig of which Eve took with her when she and Adam were driven out and which she then planted. The parent tree and its offspring flourished through the centuries, and it is from these trees that Solomon's wife cut wood to attach to the bed. The significance of the hues—white, red, and green—of the wood is related to events in the early years of sacred history: the white wood is for the virginity of the first parents, the green is for the fruitfulness denoted by the conception of Abel, and the red is for the murder of Abel by Cain. The author's careful description of this history and his meshing of different histories expand the significance of the wood on the ship and give it a richness of meaning justifying the digression made to include it. All these objects on the ship carry with them the significance of sacred and, in particular, Grail history as well as functioning to dissolve the temporal separation of the two histories. By means of them Galahad is made aware of Solomon's foreknowledge, and Solomon himself, after making the ship ready, is told by God that it will serve to inform the knight that Solomon knew of his coming: "Salemons, li derreains chevaliers de ton lignage se reposera en cest lit que tu as fet, et savra noveles de toi" (p. 225, ll. 31–32) [Solomon, the last knight of thy lineage will lie on this bed that thou hast made and will have tidings of thee (p. 235)]. Thus, these objects, besides spanning time, also provide reciprocal communication between Galahad and Solomon, enhancing their atemporal significance.

In this digression, analogy is also used as a means of connection. Figural relationships of various kinds—both contrasting and similar—are set forth by the author in his account of the legend. Eve is contrasted with the Virgin and compared with her as well: through Eve life was lost, and through the Virgin it was restored. However, Eve's carrying the twig from the Tree of Life out of the Garden was a symbol of the return to Paradise (p. 213, ll. 2–5; ll. 9–13 [pp. 223–24]). The story of the murder of Abel functions as an analogy to Judas's betrayal of Christ: "Et la mort que Abel reçut par traison a cel tens . . . senefia la mort au verai Crucifié, car par Abel fu il senefiez et par Caym fu senefiez Judas par qui il reçut mort" (p. 217, ll. 25–28) [And the death that Abel met through treachery, at the time . . . was a symbol of Christ's death upon the Cross, for Abel signified Our Lord, and Cain prefigured Judas, who brought about His death (p. 227)]. The guile of Solomon's wife is compared to that of Eve; the author states that deception and cunning are common to all women but that it is not to be wondered at, for "ne comença pas a nos, mes a nostre premiere mere" (p. 220, ll. 18–19) [this is nothing new, but dates back to the mother of us all (p. 230)]. God then contrasts Solomon's wife to the Virgin Mary, who will be of Solomon's lineage, in an effort to comfort Solomon who laments his inability, in spite of his wisdom, to get the better of his wife: "Salemon, Salemon, se de fame vint et vient tristece a home, ne t'en chaille. Car une fame sera encore dont il vendra a home greignor joie cent tanz que cest tristece n'est; et cele fame nestra de ton lignage" (p. 220, l. 32–p. 221, l. 2) [Solomon, Solomon, if sorrow came to man through woman's wiles, and comes so still, let it not trouble thee. For there shall come a woman through whom man shall know joy greater an hundred times than is this sorrow; and she shall be born of thine inheritance (p. 230)]. These are the explicit analogies drawn by the author; from them and from implied analogies, the general figural relationships can now be traced ultimately to the Grail.

The analogies to be outlined here are relationships on an atemporal plane; the connections are vertical, and thus one element does not cause the other, even if in the special world of the *Queste* all events are seen as interrelated parts of a providential design controlled by God and symbolized by the Grail. One main line of analogy is that of women. Eve is analogous to Solomon's wife in her deception, but they both have redemptive qualities as well, in that Eve is the bearer of the twig and Solomon's wife is the builder of the Miraculous Ship. And both Eve and Solomon's wife contrast with the Virgin Mary. Mary will be the means of restoration of that lost by Eve, and, coming of Solomon's lineage, will by her virtue balance the cunning of Solomon's wife. Perceval's sister is also analogous to the Virgin Mary in her purity and is imbued with redeeming qualities by her willingness to give up her life for the Leprous Lady. As spiritual instructress, Perceval's sister contrasts with Eve and Solomon's wife as temptresses. In this role she is also implicitly contrasted with Guinevere, who, as a type of Eve, serves the devil as an agent of damnation. Perceval's sister also completes the work done by Eve and Solomon's wife—planting the tree and building the ship—by explaining the significance of the ship and its objects, and by making a belt for the sword, as Solomon's wife had foreseen.

Another line of analogy leads to Galahad. Although he is not explicitly compared to Christ in this section, the numerous analogies drawn throughout the *Queste* and noted above have, by the time we reach the section on the ship, taken firm hold. Thus, the explicit analogy between Abel and Christ is very easily extended to include Galahad. Abel is a type of the Crucified Christ, and Galahad of the Redeeming Christ. As the author says, these comparisons are "non pas de hautece, mes de senefiance" (p. 217, ll. 31–32) [not in degree, but in their outward signs (p. 228)]. Yet through them we are led to see the significance of Galahad's achievement of the Grail as implicit in the great events of Christian history and as profoundly related to them.

All of the Grail's historical manifestations are brought together in the final Grail ceremonies, where they attain a simultaneity that in fact becomes ahistorical both on the literal level and on the level of meaning. Galahad does come to Mordrain, who then finally dies (p. 262, l. 20–p. 263, l. 26 [pp. 269–70]), and he does heal the Maimed King (p. 271, l. 32–p. 272, l. 7 [p. 277]). At the ceremonies at the castles of Corbenic and Sarras, Josephus is present, and at the Castle of Corbenic, Christ speaks to Galahad in His own person. All the historical manifestations have become one whole, whose true nature yet remains ineffable and inexpressible as the mysteries of the Grail.

By means of *digressio*, "bringing in first what is actually remote and altering the natural order,"[39] the author has presented meaningful juxtapositions of events, thus expanding the significance of the Grail. Through them, and the oblique views they open up, the story is enriched by historical perspective. The Grail sends its rays back into history, giving earlier events meaning, while the historical events themselves contribute partial definitions to the truth of the Grail. Like the

Smooth Flow of Forces Frankl finds to be characteristic of Gothic cathedrals, *digressio* produces the impression of an interpenetration of parts not subject to the laws of probability. Just as the structural members of a Gothic cathedral appear to soar upward without visible support, so too historical digressions expand the range of the effects of the Grail by discovering hidden connections neither causally explicit nor temporally possible. They are the workings of Providence.

INTERLACE

The Grail in the *Queste* is like Geoffrey's "little seed" from which "great harvest springs." By means of techniques derived from the rhetorical tradition, the author has elaborated on the meaning of the Grail through dynamic amplification of narrative. For purposes of examination, the function of each of the amplificatory techniques in the *Queste—interpretatio, circumlocutio,* and *digressio*—has been described separately; however, the structural cohesion of the work derives from their interrelations. These interrelations are effected by interlace.

It is generally agreed that the term *entrelacement* most accurately describes the structure of the Vulgate Cycle as a whole; it is not, however, used to the same purpose in each romance within that cycle. Interlace in the *Lancelot* Proper primarily serves to delineate adventures;[40] since most adventures demonstrate the preeminence of Lancelot as an examplar of courtly knighthood, there emerges a kind of hierarchical structure as Lancelot becomes "li meildres chevaliers del monde" (*Queste*, p. 5, 1. 27 [p. 35]) and himself the goal of numerous quests. However, this designation is valid only on an entirely terrestrial level. Without the reference to the Grail, all adventure takes place on a horizontal plane; whereas in the *Queste,* with the Grail present as constant referent, adventures have clearly distinguishable levels of meaning on a vertical axis. Interlace can thus serve either purpose: it can throw Lancelot's prowess into relief by juxtaposition with the achievements of lesser knights in the *Lancelot* Proper, or it can reveal Lancelot's failings in the spiritual realm by setting his responses to the Grail

against those of the elect knights. In the *Queste* interlace contributes to the clearly spiritual hierarchical ranking of knights
and to our perception of the spiritual significance of that hierarchy. By means of interlace, meaningful juxtapositions
emerge that are neither causal—Galahad does not cause Lancelot's failure—nor explicit but whose significances arise from
formal patterns perceived by the reader through what Vinaver
has called "the gift of formal vision."[41]

   This "gift of formal vision" allows us to reinterpret the entire
Vulgate Cycle, and especially the *Lancelot* Proper, by the
Queste. Just as within the *Queste* itself new insight into the
nature of the Grail forces retrospective understanding of previous episodes, so too knowledge of the Grail compels reevaluation of the proliferation of chivalric adventures in the
Lancelot Proper. This is the result of the concomitance of interlace with artificial order.[42] According to Geoffrey of Vinsauf,
artificial order is that which "advances along the pathway of
art" (*PN*, p. 18), rather than following nature. It is obvious that
an interlaced narrative is the result of an imposition of order
designed to serve art rather than nature. John Leyerle, in his
discussion of the structure of *Beowulf*, describes the effective-
ness of interlace to convey the ineffable:

This design reveals the meaning of coincidence, the recurrence of
human behaviour, and the circularity of the medium itself—the interlace structure. It allows for the intersection of narrative events without
regard for their distance in chronological time and shows the interrelated significances of episodes without the need for any explicit comment by the poet. The significance of the connections is left for the
audience to work out for itself.[43]

What Leyerle says is clearly pertinent to the convergence of
meanings in the *Queste*; but it also describes the means by
which, on an allegorical level, the Grail gives meaning to
events in the *Lancelot* Proper. On the level of the narrative, the
adventures of the *Lancelot* Proper gain their significance and
motivation from interlace in the way described by Vinaver and
Leyerle, and progress forward in chronological—or natural—

order. On this level the story also converges on the *Queste* and the *Mort Artu*. The order is radically altered, however, on the allegorical level imposed by the presence of the Grail. Because of the *Queste's* centrality to the entire cycle—it is the high altar, as it were, of the cathedral—it throws its meaning backward and forward; all must be referred to it. In the light of the Grail, the values and ideals of the *Lancelot* Proper undergo reevaluation, and in the *Queste* but not before, they can be seen as morally bankrupt. Thus, interlace, with the artificial order it produces, creates meanings only possible by such formal patterning.

By means of interlace the *Queste* itself also presents its meaning through formal patterning. Vinaver has said, "any exploration of form is a search for meaning."[44] This is especially true for analysis of the *Queste*. The meaning of the work lies in the Grail, an object whose essence is partially unveiled by means of its manifestations in description and narrative. What we know of the Grail is reflected in the structure of the work it has produced. Frankl's concept of the style of Partiality describes structural members that appear fragmentary and interdependent while contributing to a larger whole. The *Queste* also presents us at every point with fragmentary aspects of the Grail. Its *synecdochic* mode permits the partial derivation of the whole from its parts. These parts of the meaning of the Grail result from the use of techniques of amplification to represent the Grail in romance. The narrative resulting from this application is made more "partial" and more complex in the coherence and interdependence of its parts through the interlace of these techniques with one another.

As we have seen, *interpretatio* functions in the *Queste* in a manner corresponding to the principle of Spatial Division in a Gothic cathedral. Spatial Division describes the impression gained by viewing a Gothic cathedral that one is confronted with divisions of a whole. In the *Queste* each knight's total experience in his quest for the Grail ranks him in the hierarchy of knights. This whole is divided into episodes by *interpretatio*, repetitions that are "varied and yet the same." Through these repetitions we come to know part of the meaning of the Grail as manifest in the adventures of a given knight. As the discussion of the Bors section illustrated, the repetition of meaning on various levels—real history, dreams, visions, exposition—is incremental; each manifestation leads to greater understanding: "Allegorical reading is very well served by this opportunity to realize, realize, and realize again, the full import of something we can only lamely point to by its abstract name."[45] The "full import," however, is gained gradually through the interrelation of fragmentary manifestations. Meaningful connections leading to understanding result from the artful interlace of the repetitions. Bors's dream of the two lilies and the rotten wood is related on the level of significance to his decision to rescue the maiden rather than Lyonel. The dream does not cause the action; yet each repetition provides insight into the meaning of Bors's response to the Grail through interlaced significances. *Interpretatio* serves to define the experience of each of the exemplary knights in the same way; however, the individual knights' quests are thrown into greater relief by the interlace of each with the others as *circumlocutio*.

Circumlocutio describes the quest structure of this romance. The individual quests of the exemplary knights—Gawain, Lancelot, Bors, Perceval, and Galahad—constitute so many "winding paths" that define achievement of the Grail. As Tuve noted, "We should never understand the purport of Galahad's actions or take in the quality of his single-minded fidelity, if we did not come to it by way of the several varied and flawed forms of devotion which the other questers exhibit."[46] This use of *circumlocutio* parallels the structural principle of Gothic architecture that Frankl calls Diagonality. The term describes the impossibility at any place in a Gothic cathedral to obtain frontal views; rather, all views are diagonal and oblique, creating the impression of incompleteness. The views created by the use of *circumlocutio* in the *Queste* are also oblique and diagonal because, although each knight's experience of the Grail contributes to our knowledge of what is necessary to achieve it, each is incomplete and meaningless without the others. For example, a given section devoted to Lancelot does not in itself contain all we need to know of what is happening to him. Comparisons are drawn between Lancelot and the others, and through such interconnections, our understanding of his experience is enlarged and refined. Interlace provides the means for establishing the points of connection between the parts produced by *circumlocutio*. The sections presenting each knight's adventures are not merely set next to each other; they are entwined throughout the responses each makes to the Grail. Tuve's description of what occurs is again apt:

But events connected by entrelacement are not juxtaposed; they are interlaced, and when we get back to our first character he is not where we left him as we finished his episode, but in the place of psychological state or condition of meaningfulness to which he has been pulled by the events occurring in following episodes written about someone else.[47]

Although Lancelot's first section ends with his avowal to mend his ways and abandon his former sinful life, when we return to him again we are aware of how difficult his road will be because we have in the meantime seen Perceval's responses to the Grail made on the basis of his simple faith. Having observed Perceval's complete trust in God when abandoned on an island of wild beasts, we appreciate Lancelot's inability to give up trust in his own prowess for the spiritual obstacle that it is. Lancelot has not changed, but by means of the diagonal views provided by the interlace of parts, our vision of him has.

Interspersed among the adventures of the knights are *digressiones*, or the narrative episodes relating the history of the Grail; by themselves they indicate the significance of the Grail in the Christian past. However, they do not stand alone but, as digressions, are interlaced with the "subject," the present Grail adventures—which are already interlaced with each other—thus increasing the density of the design and the number of partial manifestations of the meaning of the Grail.

The pattern drawn by interlacing the digressions with the adventures in the *Queste* produces dimensions of meaning for the Grail beyond its circumscribed significances for the Arthurian world, yet the digressions interact with these significances and thus expand them. The inclusion of excerpts from the legends of Joseph of Arimathea, Mordrain, Nascien, the Maimed King and their Grail experiences lends import to the Grail by increasing the historical range of its effects. Because all that happens to these characters in relation to the Grail is preparatory in nature, the inclusion of these excerpts concentrates that history on the moment of Galahad's achievement of the Grail. Thus, past history and present moment become one through Providence. The effect of temporal interpenetration produced by *digressio* is similar to what Frankl calls the Smooth Flow of Forces in Gothic architecture; the impression produced by each principle is fluidity and freely flowing lines of force. As a Gothic cathedral appears to defy natural laws in its upward sweep, so the *Queste* incorporates within its structure analogical and figural motivations that defy temporal limitations.

Because the historical digressions are interlaced with adventures of the Grail knights, the meaning of the Grail is unveiled on two levels simultaneously. While each progressive section devoted to the adventures of an individual knight increases our knowledge of what is required of one who would attain the Grail, through its "echoes and anticipations" interlaced with other sections, at the same time the providential history of the Grail is gradually revealed to us through digressions interlaced within these sections. Hence, our discovery of the historical import of the Grail grows concomitantly with our understanding of its effects on its seekers. By the time of the two digressions within the Perceval section—one relating the history of the three tables and the other the story of God's punishment of King Mordrain's presumption—we are able to understand their significance for this quest because we have already accompanied Galahad, Gawain, and Lancelot through the initial stages of their quests and have learned some of its moral requirements.

Similarly, the digression on the Tree of Life, which integrates into the Grail quest the story of Solomon and his wife and even Adam and Eve, occurs when the testing of the knights is complete. The ranking of the knights at that point is clear, as is the justification for the resultant hierarchy; because we understand this, we are vouchsafed the knowledge of the Grail implicated throughout Christian history. The Grail thus gains meaning for us as our knowledge of its effects broadens. By the end of the Tree of Life section, we know everything necessary for a proper understanding of the significance of the Grail ceremonies that conclude the romance. What we have learned has been possible through interlace. As Leyerle states, "[Interlace] allows for the intersection of narrative events without regard for their distance in chronological time and shows the interrelated significances of events without the need for any explicit comment by the poet."[48]

Frankl observes that one can understand the meaning of architecture through the "symbolism of form." Similarly, Focillon states:

Form has a meaning—but it is a meaning entirely its own, a personal and specific value that must not be confused with the attributes we impose upon it. Form has a significance and form is open to interpretation.[49]

The above analysis has demonstrated that the meaning of the *Queste* can be known by defining its form. Its meaning, however, is unveiled only partially and therein lies what we can know of its meaning; as God's *secrees*, its total meaning, like God, transcends human comprehension.[50] Galahad, who achieves a true vision, cannot say what he has seen, and it transports him beyond mortal life. By showing Galahad unable to express the truth of the Grail, the author makes it clear that it is also beyond his own ability to translate through words.[51] As readers, we accept this, since by the time of the final revelation to Galahad, the author has already shown us that the structure of his romance permits only a partial understanding of the Grail. As Focillon says, "form is open to interpretation," and by presenting what we can know of the Grail through fragmentary, interdependent parts, the author states its partial nature for us. To identify the Grail precisely is to impose attributes upon it that both limit our understanding and are not indicated by the work. It is also to ignore what even the structure of the work tells us—its partiality.

Just as Frankl's formal concepts defining Gothic architecture overlap with each other to produce the impression of partiality, the techniques of amplification used by the author of the *Queste* are not as strictly separated as this discussion of them, for the purposes of clarity, may tend to imply. *Interpretatio* does most accurately describe the repetition, on various levels, of each knight's experience of the Grail; however, *circumlocutio*—the unwinding by circuitous paths of the adventures of all the knights—also partakes of *interpretatio*, since each knight's experience does repeat that of the others, although on different hierarchical or model levels. *Digressio* in the *Queste* conforms closely to the definition of that term; yet many of these digressions also operate as *interpretationes*, repeating from various perspectives the story of the Grail's coming to Great Britain with Joseph of Arimathea. All of this, however, enhances our perception of the density of the *Queste's* structure and underscores the partial nature of what is revealed to us of the Grail's meaning. Because of the complexity of this interlaced design, the *Queste* can support countless rereadings, for new and meaningful associations may be discovered with each. A Gothic cathedral reveals new vistas with every visit, yet all of them express aspects of the high altar and radiate from it. So, too, do all the parts of the *Queste*, mysterious in themselves, relate to the Grail as parts of the design it has created. And like the configuration of forms in a Gothic cathedral, it is a rich and beautiful design.

CHAPTER IV

Abbreviation and Meaning in Malory's
Tale of the Sankgreal

We have seen that the *Queste del Saint Graal* articulates its meaning through amplification; the meaning of the Grail is elaborated in parts in a manner analogous to the structural principles of a Gothic cathedral. The style of Partiality characterizing Gothic architecture is paralleled in the rhetorical tradition by the *synecdochic* mode, wherein the whole is inferred from the parts. Thus, the meaning of the work, which is the meaning of the Grail, is only revealed in parts which increase our understanding but never state explicitly nor totally the nature or meaning of that which is sought. Dynamic amplification in the *Queste* elaborates on the meaning of the Grail through the narrative it produces as quests, these quests in turn revealing various aspects of the Grail's meaning through the multitude of varied responses to it by different knights.

Malory's purpose, unlike that of his source, was not the partial unveiling of the attributes of an ineffable Grail. In his work the meaning of the Grail is known from the beginning: it is the Eucharistic vessel. As we have seen, all his excisions and alterations of the static amplification of the Grail in his source demonstrate this. Therefore, the narrative caused by the Grail in his work serves a purpose other than to reveal the vessel's meaning. This purpose can best by discovered by an examination of that narrative through the compositional techniques of abbreviation.

RESTRICTION

Geoffrey of Vinsauf taught that to abbreviate, one must "prune away" the devices for amplification. Malory eliminated those devices used by the author of the *Queste* to elaborate his work; we shall begin by examining Malory's treatment of *digressio*.

All eight historical digressions in the *Queste* serve to expand the meaning of the Grail in time and to add a larger historical dimension to the present Arthurian moment. The actual achievement of the Grail gains in significance by means of historical preparation for the event. Correspondingly, the historical digressions, because they are often prompted by the need to explain a present event or object, also collapse time, since that which calls for explanation continues to exist in the present. Thus, all time becomes one in order to concentrate on the mystery of Galahad's achievement of the Grail.

Malory suppresses, as far as possible, historical digression. His adaptations of the narrative, like the changes we noted in his representation of the Grail itself, are meaningful and appropriate to the narrower focus he brings to the Grail history.

The first historical digression in the *Queste*, prompted by Galahad's desire to know about the shield the White Knight has given him, is left largely intact by Malory (Q. p. 32, l. 6–p. 35, l. 12 [pp. 58–60]; M. p. 879, l. 19–p. 881, l. 21); he follows his source in relating the conversion of Mordrain/Evelach by Josephus and the subsequent conversion of Britain. The episode in Malory is almost an exact translation of the French, except for a few omissions, but these alter its emphasis significantly. Malory does link past and present by the prediction that Galahad shall be the possessor of Josephus's shield; how-

ever, he eliminates the *Queste*'s stress on predestination as
well as its emphasis on punishment for those who presume to
bear the shield but are not worthy to do so. Malory follows his
source when he has Josephus say, "and never shall no man
beare thys shylde aboute hys necke but he shall repente hit,
unto the tyme that Galahad, the good knyght, beare hit" (M.
p. 881, ll. 9–12). But he omits the stern warning in his source
directed at those who may wish to take up the shield but who
do not have Galahad's perfect virtue and thus are not worthy
to receive it (Q. p. 34, ll. 27–32 [p. 69]). Furthermore, in the
Queste the White Knight concludes by reiterating Galahad's
predestined role and reemphasizing the dire fate suffered by
other knights who presumptuously attempted to achieve this
adventure. In Malory the knight finishes his story without
giving this warning. Malory obviously does not wish to take
up the predestined nature of Galahad's Grail achievement;
this is not surprising, given Malory's conception of the Grail as
potentially attainable by all worthy men. His retention of this
digression depends more on its value as a simple explanation
of the origin of the shield than on the attempt of the *Queste* to
give special portent to the events just beginning. It is to Malory
an "adventure" more chivalric than sacred.[1]

Malory drastically reduces the second digression, Perceval's
aunt's response to his question about the mysterious knight
who came to court (Galahad). Malory not only shortens her
instructions (Q. p. 74, l. 20–p. 79, l. 3 [pp. 97–101]; M. p. 906,
l. 15–p. 907, l. 6); he also leaves out all the figural references to
events in Christian history. In the *Queste* Perceval's aunt relates the history of the three tables: The Table of the Last
Supper, the Table of the Holy Grail and Joseph of Arimathea,
and the Round Table. The analogy among the three tables
establishes Galahad as a type of Christ and draws together
Christian history to focus on the moment of Galahad's even-
tual achievement of the Grail. Moreover, in the *Queste* Perceval's aunt explicitly identifies Galahad as a type of Christ (Q. p.
78, ll. 21–23 [p. 100]). Malory, however, eliminates any sug-
gestion that Galahad is to be compared to Christ and in fact
makes no mention at all of the Table of the Last Supper or the

Table of the Grail, thus leaving out references to both Joseph of Arimathea and Christ. What remains in Malory is a brief account of Merlin's establishment of the Round Table and his prediction that only Galahad can occupy the "Syge Perelous."

Because Malory has rejected the entire allegorical structure of this digression as found in his source, he has reduced the episode to the literal and immediate Arthurian present. But since his main concern is with the actions of men in this world and during this particular quest, his treatment of the digression seems appropriate. He clearly does not wish to weaken the significance of the present moment by introducing subtle relationships with the past. The fact that he retains Perceval's aunt's remarks on the joys of chivalric brotherhood, even to the exclusion of home and family, also suggests that his concern lies with historical chivalry rather than doctrinal allegory:

For all the worlde, crystenyd and hethyn, repayryth unto the Rounde Table, and whan they ar chosyn to be of the felyshyp of the Rounde Table they thynke hemselff more blessed and more in worship than they had gotyn halff the worlde. (M. p. 906, ll. 17–21)

As we see, Malory systematically eliminates narrative that takes attention away from his major interest: how earthly knights, with the Christian vocation that knighthood implies, ought to act to be worthy of seeing the Eucharist unveiled in this world.

In the third digression the story of the Maimed King is told to Perceval by a priest; Malory retains only the bare outline of the episode as it stands in his source (Q. p. 83, l. 21–p. 86, l. 32 [pp. 105–8]; M. p. 908, l. 14–p. 909, l. 2). He omits the retelling of Mordrain's rescue of Josephus from prison and the fact that while in prison Josephus and his followers were sustained entirely by the Holy Grail. Rather, he moves directly to the unique feature of this retelling, Mordrain's overwhelming desire to be near the Grail: "and ever he was bysy to be thereas the Sankgreall was" (M. p. 908, ll. 20–21). He relates God's punishment of Mordrain for having drawn closer to the Grail than he ought and God's promise to Mordrain that he will in time be healed by the good knight Galahad; in Malory as well as in his source, Mordrain has lived four hundred years awaiting his healing. However, this is all Malory relates; again, he rejects far more than he retains. He leaves out a great deal of historical detail surrounding Josephus's entry into Britain and the circumstances of his imprisonment and rescue. To Malory this would appear to be needless repetition of what he had related previously. In the *Queste* the repetition of Grail history with new details added to each retelling gives added significance to the final achieving of the Grail; for Malory only what is new in each digression seems worth recording.

Besides eliminating historical repetition, Malory also omits in this digression details that do not fit his conception either of the Grail or of the quest for it (Q. p. 85, ll. 13–15 [p. 106]). He conceives of the Grail as humanly comprehensible; thus, he carefully avoids the statement of its ineffability found in his source. Malory further leaves out of this digression analogies between Galahad and Christ. In the *Queste* Simeon's waiting for the infant Christ is likened to Mordrain's waiting for Galahad (p. 86, ll. 29–32 [pp. 107–8]). The analogy serves to link figurally past and present, while at the same time emphasizing the significance of Galahad's predestined role. Malory totally eliminates this part of the digression. Retaining it would have lessened the impact of present, immediate events and would also have reduced the potential for achieving the Grail for those who are not predestined.

Malory's treatment of the fourth digression, the hermit's explanation of Lancelot's dream, entirely alters its character (Q. p. 134, l. 13–p. 138, l. 8 [pp. 151–54]; M. p. 929, l. 28–p. 930, l. 18). In the *Queste* the hermit's explanation of Lancelot's dream by means of a dream of Mordrain's causes different historical perspectives to merge. The two dreams—in terms of narrative—take place at the same time. The destined achievement of Galahad thus transcends time and causes history to collapse. The hermit in the *Queste* begins his interpretation of Lancelot's dream by relating the history of Joseph of Arimathea. Malory reduces this to one sentence and then has the hermit go on to interpret Lancelot's dream with no mention of

Mordrain's. The effect is to focus attention on Lancelot's own moral development. These emphases are also evident in Malory's handling of the hermit's interpretation of the dream. Malory follows his source in listing Lancelot's ancestors and their virtues, although in a far shorter version. When the hermit comes to Lancelot's grandfather, he says, "and he was as worthy a man as thou arte" (M. p. 930, ll. 7–8), a statement not in Malory's source. It demonstrates his continued effort to stress the present as well as his general tendency to enhance Lancelot's significance in the story. Malory's rehabilitation of Lancelot is further borne out by his reducing to a short sentence a large section in his source on Galahad's virtues, while making an addition of his own:

And thou ought to thanke God more than ony othir man lyvyng, for of a synner erthely thou hast no pere as in knyghthode nother never shall have. But lytyll thanke hast thou yevyn to God for all the grete vertuys that God hath lente the. (M. p. 930, ll. 14–18)

Although these words are critical of Lancelot, they do not keep the harsh condemnation in the *Queste*; and their praise of his chivalry and virtues is not found there.[2] By omitting the explanation of Mordrain's dream and much other historical material, and by adding these words to the judgment of Lancelot, Malory radically alters the focus of the digression, placing it where he believes it belongs: on "synners erthely" in their struggle to become worthy of succeeding in the quest.

The next three digressions, explanations by Perceval's sister of the histories behind the objects bearing inscriptions on the Miraculous Ship, are not substantially changed by Malory, although they are shortened. Nonetheless, their significance is altered. In the *Queste* these digressions serve to link past and present by means of the objects themselves (sword hilt, blade, and scabbard) and also through the histories of those who attempted to possess these objects without having been designated for them or being worthy of possessing them. The digressions thereby demonstrate Galahad's role as elect knight, since all those who aspired to take the objects, however worthy, were punished by God for their presumption. Thus, the explanations reveal that the time has come for their predestined owner to take possession and also that the final achievement of the Grail is drawing near. However, since Malory leaves out many of the linking phrases between the digressions, which indicate why an explanation is necessary, the stories stand as interesting but isolated units—to which Galahad can only respond, "In the name of God, damesell!" (M. p. 990, l. 15). Perceval's sister does in fact introduce these digressions abruptly, prompted by nothing (M. p. 988, l. 14; M. p. 989, l. 33). Malory perhaps finds these histories interesting as tales of adventure. But it is clear that they serve him more as examples of God's punishment for disobedience than as narrative expansions on the Grail's meaning and history.

Malory's most dramatic abbreviation of the digressions in his source is the Legend of the Tree of Life (Q. p. 210, l. 29–p. 226, l. 7 [pp. 222–35]; M. p. 990, l. 22–p. 994, l. 16). First, he does not follow his source in making this digression a separate section narrated by the author; rather, he has Perceval's sister relate the legend to Perceval, Bors, and Galahad in explanation of the varied colors of the wood in the spindles of the bed on the ship. The digression thus follows the pattern of Perceval's sister's explanations of the other objects on the ship and is not set apart as special and perhaps more sacred, as in the *Queste*. Second, Malory greatly alters the focus of this digression. In the *Queste* two-thirds of the legend is devoted to Adam and Eve and the story of the Tree of Life, while one-third relates the story of Solomon and his wife and the building of the Miraculous Ship. In Malory, however, only two short paragraphs, approximately one-fifth of the digression, deal with Adam and Eve, while the rest of the narrative centers on Solomon and his wife.

Malory's abbreviation of the Adam and Eve section removes all the *Queste*'s doctrinal amplifications: the distinctions between maidenhood and virginity, the analogy between Cain and Judas, and the sacred symbolism attached to events and objects. Instead, he simply relates what happened: that Eve brought a twig from the Tree of Life out of the Garden of Eden and planted it, and that it changed from white when Adam and Eve were virgins, to green when Abel was conceived, to red when Cain killed Abel. For Malory it is enough simply to account for the wood in the bed. To this end he excised as far as possible amplificatory material, retaining only the historical narrative necessary to explain events in the present.

Further evidence of Malory's use of the *Queste*'s digressions only as historical background can be found in his alterations of the Solomon part of the Legend of the Tree of Life. In the *Queste* Solomon's chief concern is that Galahad should be aware that Solomon knew of his coming; hence, Solomon's wife suggests building the ship as a sign to Galahad, and the ship becomes the logical solution to a problem. In Malory, however, while Solomon is simply pondering what might be the name of the last knight of his lineage, his wife suddenly says, "I shall lette make a shippe of the beste wood and moste durable that ony man may fynde" (M. p. 992, ll. 10–11). In the light of Malory's source, this is a *non sequitur*, but for Malory it is an adequate introduction to the ship-building episode, since for him the important thing is how the ship on which Galahad, Perceval, and Bors have boarded came into existence. That Malory is not concerned with communication between the centuries can also be seen in God's final message to Solomon when the ship is completed: "Salamon, the laste knyght of thy kynred shall reste in thys bedde" (M. p. 994, ll. 13–14). This would not have satisfied the Solomon of the *Queste*, to whom God speaks the same words but adds, "et savra noveles de toi" (Q. p. 225, l. 32) [and will have tidings of thee (p. 235)]. Malory's omission of the message that Galahad will learn that Solomon knew of him destroys the careful merging of historical moments found in the *Queste* and creates a temporal separation better adapted to Malory's intent.

The changes Malory makes in the entire Tree of Life section excise the figural interpenetrations from real historical explanations. The communication between Solomon and Galahad is removed. Similarly, the elaborate analogies found in Malory's source no longer function in his adaptation. Because of the many comments by the author of the *Queste* on the nature of women, we are led in that work to make various figural connections: Eve is to Solomon's wife and Guinevere as Mary is to Perceval's sister. These analogical relationships draw events into an atemporal pattern, where all history focuses on the moment of Galahad's achievement of the Grail. Furthermore, in the *Queste* Perceval's sister completes the work begun by Eve and Solomon's wife—planting the tree and building the ship—by making a belt for the sword as Solomon's wife had foreseen. However, in Malory Solomon's wife does not know how the sword will gain a new belt. When Solomon complains about the meanness of the hempen belt his wife has attached to the sword, she says:

Sir, wyte you welle that I have none so hyghe a thynge whych were worthy to susteyne soo hyghe a swerde. And a mayde shall brynge other knyghtes thereto, but I wote not whan hit shall be ne what tyme. (M. p. 993, ll. 1–4)

Therefore, when Perceval's sister does make a belt for the sword from her own hair, the significance of her action as the fulfillment of past prophecy and the completion of past labor is lost. The other analogical line found in the *Queste*—Abel as Christ as Galahad—is also eliminated by Malory. Previous to this section in the *Queste*, Galahad is often compared to Christ; and within this section we are told that Abel prefigures Christ. Thus, all three are bound together in an analogical relationship. However, since Malory up to this point in the work has left out all references to Galahad as a type of Christ, and eliminates from this section the analogy between Abel and Christ, there is no typological connection among them in his work. The entire episode becomes simply a marvelous adventure, and Galahad remains as the worthiest of knights, foretold by God but lacking profound underpinnings in sacred history. For Malory historical epochs remain discrete.

It is clear that Malory, following Geoffrey's instruction on abbreviation, has "pruned away" much of the *digressiones* used by the author of the *Queste* to amplify and elaborate his work. It is also clear that Malory's elimination of much of the historical digressive material found in his source is not without purpose. His primary concern is the "material at hand," and he thus chooses from the "actually remote" only that which is still necessary to clarify present events. Further, Malory significantly reduces the impression that there are any digressions at all. Because his digressions are so radically shortened, they become a part of present dialogue rather than lengthy, isolated narrations of the "actually remote." This is most clearly seen in Malory's alteration of the Tree of Life section, where the entire digression is related by Perceval's sister, rather than by the author/narrator as it is in the *Queste*. This mode of telling in combination with the many excisions noted above transforms the legend into present material. By abbreviation of the digressive material in his source and narrowing of the meaning of the Grail in comparison to that work, Malory abandons the *synecdochic* mode, wherein the whole is derived from the parts, and the entire impression is one of Partiality. Instead, he reduces and narrows those parts in an attempt to construct a whole whose meaning is centralized in the present and the comprehensible.

AVOIDANCE OF REPETITION

Malory's consistent tendency away from the style of Partiality found in his source can also be seen in his avoidance of *interpretatio* (repetition). In the *Queste interpretatio* dictates that the experience of each knight in the quest be repeated in parts and in various modes—adventure, vision, dream, explication. These parts are fragmentary, each requiring the others to approach full significance. In the discussion of the *Queste* above, Bors's quest was used as an example of the way *interpretatio* functions in the work. However, for Malory we will examine selected examples from the book as a whole; for although the sequence of adventures, visions, dreams, and explication within a given adventure is not often altered by him, the overall focus is. To a large extent Malory eliminates the level of explication—what the author of the *Queste* calls *senefiance*—from the experience of each knight but retains the adventures, visions, and dreams. What little explication he does keep conforms to his new conception of the work.

The first example of Malory's abbreviation of *interpretatio* is in Galahad's adventure of the tomb. Malory relates it much as does his source. Galahad is led by monks to a tomb, from which issues a voice that causes men to lose their strength; the monks believe the tomb harbors a fiend. The knight's presence causes the fiend to lose his power, and the spell is broken. It is in the interpretation of this adventure by one of the monks that Malory departs from his source.

The interpretation of this adventure in the *Queste* is far longer than in Malory (Q. p. 37, l. 23–p. 40, l. 1 [pp. 63–65]; M. p. 882, ll. 28–35) and carries a great deal more symbolic weight. The French Galahad asks for an interpretation of the adventures associated with the tomb, and the monk replies by telling him the significance of the tomb, the body within it, and the voice issuing from it. The interpretation includes an account of the Incarnation, the sinfulness of the Jews, and the Passion; the monk says explicitly, "Einsi poez vos veoir en ceste aventure la senefiance de la Passion Jhesucrist et la semblance de son avenement" (Q. p. 39, ll. 19–21) [Thus the adventure shows forth the meaning of the Passion of Jesus Christ, while at the same time it symbolizes His coming (p. 65)]. Along with the doctrinal meanings the monk attaches to the adventure, and interwoven with them, are numerous analogies between Christ and Galahad in their redemptive roles (Q. p. 38, ll. 15–21 [p. 64]), giving the adventure a significance far beyond the literal level. The interpretation thus incorporates both doctrinal and figural meanings.

Malory, however, completely eliminates the figural meanings and retains very little doctrine. His Galahad does not ask for an interpretation; the monk simply begins speaking:

Sir, I shall telle you what betokenyth of that ye saw in the tombe. Sir, that that coverde the body, hit betokenyth the duras of the worlde, and the grete synne that oure Lorde founde in the worlde. For there was suche wrecchydnesse that the fadir loved nat the sonne, nother the sonne loved nat the fadir. And that was one of the causys that oure

Lorde toke fleysh and bloode of a clene maydyn; for oure synnes were
so grete at that tyme that well-nyghe all was wyckednesse. (M. p. 882,
11. 28–35)

Malory has retained only the interpretation of the tomb, leaving out that of the body and the voice, and has abbreviated the
meaning of the tomb as found in his source. Although everything that Malory's monk says can be found in the *Queste*, the
parts that Malory uses are so much abridged that his source's
context and indeed the entire allegorical structure are lost,
including the highly spiritual *senefiance* attached to the adventure in the *Queste*. Only the moral intent of Christ's coming
remains.

This adaptation conforms to Malory's consistent effort to
confine his work to the literal plane. He has avoided the figural
level so pervasive in the *Queste* in order that Galahad may be
seen as the best of earthly knights, not as a type of Christ. He
has taken from his source only what he felt was relevant to his
own work, that for the wickedness of the world, Christ was
sent to save man. Since Malory's quest involves the efforts of
men to experience the Eucharist, the recognition of good and
bad behavior is pertinent, while doctrinal allegory and figural
identification are not.

Another example of Malory's elimination of the allegorical
level from his narrative occurs when Lancelot first meets a
hermit and asks for confession. Before hearing his confession,
the hermit asks Lancelot his name; when he learns who the
knight is, he is astonished to find Lancelot so wretched. In the
Queste this leads to an enumeration by the hermit of the gifts
God bestowed on Lancelot, a telling of the Parable of the
Talents, and much adjuration to turn to confession and repentance by which means God may again count the knight as one
of His own (Q. p. 63, l. 13–p. 64, l. 25 [pp. 87–88]). Malory
totally eliminates the Parable of the Talents and abbreviates
the direct exhortations to Lancelot, combining them with the
hermit's catalogue of Lancelot's gifts and accomplishments:

Sir . . . ye ought to thanke God more than ony knyght lyvynge, for

He hath caused you to have more worldly worship than ony knyght that ys now lyvynge. And for youre presumpcion to take uppon you in dedely synne for to be in Hys presence, where Hys fleyssh and Hys blood was, which caused you ye myght nat se hyt with youre worldly yen, for He woll not appere where such synners bene but if hit be unto their grete hurte other unto their shame. And there is no knyght now lyvynge that ought to yelde God so grete thanke os ye, for He hath yevyn you beaute, bownte, semelynes, and grete strengthe over all other knyghtes. And therefore ye ar the more beholdyn unto God than ony other man to love Hym and drede Hym, for youre strengthe and youre manhode woll litill avayle you and God be agaynste you. (M. p. 896, l. 29–p. 897, l. 7)

This passage includes direct reference to Lancelot's inability to respond to the presence of the Grail,[3] a reference not found at that place in his source. It is clear that Malory sees the hermit's role as moral counselor, not as doctrinal exegete. For Malory the Parable of the Talents is unnecessary because it is Lancelot's own talents and his misuse of them that are of importance. He relates this misuse of talents to Lancelot's impotence before the Grail not in order to delineate the abstract quality of sin but to show the effects of sin on Lancelot's quest for the Grail.

In the Perceval section Malory eliminates allegory altogether from the good man's explanation of Perceval's narrow escape from the devil disguised as a beautiful maiden. In the *Queste* (Q. p. 113, l. 1–p. 114, l. 23 [pp. 131–32]) the good man carefully explicates the adventure, relating it to Satan's Fall and the sin of Adam and Eve. He says that the battle the maiden referred to was the battle for men's souls, her tent signified the world, the sun was to be read as Jesus, and her request that Perceval come into her tent and rest signified the devil's attempt to make man forget to work toward the day of judgment. The entire allegorical structure is removed from Malory's abbreviation of this interpretation:

Than he tolde sir Percivale how oure Lord Jesu Cryste bete hym oute of hevyn for hys synne, whycch was the moste bryghtist angell of hevyn, and therefore he loste hys heritaige. "And that was the champion that thou fought withall, whych had overcom the, had nat the grace of God bene." (M. p. 920, ll. 3–11)

In the *Queste* doctrinal explication is necessary because only those events that have allegorical significance count as *aventure*; they are granted only to those who are spiritually worthy of them and thus indicate that very worthiness. Hence, Perceval's perfect faith allows him to have a meaningful adventure and to escape Satan's trap. For Malory, however, it is the narrowness of the escape that is of paramount interest; thus, he omits the allegory and adds, "Now, sir Percivale, beware and take this for an insample" (p. 920, l. 12). The adventure has become a moral example of the dangers of wrong behavior.

That Malory does not wish this explanation to go beyond the level of the secular is evident also by his omission of Perceval's recognition of the good man as Christ Himself. In the *Queste* after the explication of his adventure, Perceval says: "et se je l'osoie dire, je diroie que vos estes li Pains vis qui descent des ciex, dont nus ne menjue dignement qui pardurablement ne vive" (Q. p. 115, ll. 11–13) [Indeed, if I dared speak the words, I would say you are the Living Bread that comes down from heaven, which is a pledge of everlasting life to all who partake worthily thereof (p. 133)], whereupon the good man vanishes and a voice from the sky informs Perceval that he has conquered and must now enter the ship to await Bors and Galahad and the final Grail adventures.

To see God's secrets *apertement* in the Grail is the goal of the *Queste*, and Perceval's recognition of God reveals him as one of the elect. However, since Malory's emphasis is on right behavior rather than knowledge and the goal of his quest is the Eucharist, not the revelation of the Grail's meaning, Perceval's recognition of God at this point would be inappropriate. Thus, after the good man has told Perceval to beware and to take this adventure as a warning, Malory says, "And than the good man vanysshed. Than sir Percivale toke his armys and entirde into the shippe, and so he departed from thens" (M. p. 920, ll. 13–15). Although the identity of the good man remains obscure in Malory, his vanishing is treated so perfunctorily that it in fact raises no questions.

The second Lancelot section contains another significant example of Malory's excision of doctrinal meaning. When a hermit asks Lancelot what he seeks and the knight replies that he is seeking the adventures of the Holy Grail, the hermit says:

Well, . . . seke ye hit ye may well, but thoughe hit were here ye shall have no power to se hit, no more than a blynde man that sholde se a bryght swerde. And that ys longe on youre synne, and ellys ye were more abeler than ony man lyvynge. (M. p. 927, ll. 12–16)

Through the first sentence Malory is exactly translating his source; however, his second sentence is an extremely terse rendering of the major theme of a long sermon in the *Queste* (Q. p. 123, l. 5–p. 128, l. 15 [pp. 140–45]). In this sermon the hermit points out the virtues that formerly inhered in Lancelot —*virginité, humilité, soffrance, droiture, charité*—elaborating on the abstract qualities of each. He then relates how Satan beguiled Lancelot through Guinevere, just as Adam, Solomon, Samson, and Absalon had been deceived by women. From that time Lancelot's virtues were weakened; however, because God had endowed him so richly, he still retained enough of them to perform great feats. The hermit then elaborates on the meaning of the quest: "Car la Queste n'est mie de terrianes choses, mes de celestielx" (Q. p. 127, ll. 10–11) [For this is no Quest for earthly things, but those of heaven (p. 144)], and he likens the Parable of the Wedding Feast to the quest for the Grail.

This entire sermon is omitted by Malory. For him the catalogue of Lancelot's virtues can be adequately summed up by, "and ellys ye were more abeler than ony man lyvynge." Malory is not concerned with the qualities of the particular virtues. Similarly, "and that ys longe on youre synne" is sufficient to explain Lancelot's inability to see the Grail; the history of his love for Guinevere and the analogies with Adam, Samson, Solomon and Absalon are unnecessary for Malory.

He likewise omits the analogy between the Wedding Feast

parable and the quest for the Grail. At this point in the story, it is already clear that one must be worthy and prepared in order to achieve the quest. Again, Malory eliminates what for him is redundancy. His compositional principles are not those of the *Queste*, where repetition of the same thing in diverse ways adds to its meaning and expands its range of significance, which is of course the basis of medieval amplification. In this case likening the quest for the Grail to the Parable of the Wedding Feast adds to its significance derived from biblical tradition and contributes to establishing the quest in sacred history. But because Malory is attempting to confine his story to the Arthurian world and to find in chivalry itself the moral qualities necessary to attain the Grail, he omits what he feels to be extraneous material. This is abbreviation, the removal of those devices that contribute to amplification, in this case *interpretatio* (repetition).

These are the major examples of Malory's elimination of repetition. The tendency is, however, pervasive throughout his work. He omits Perceval's long prayer, wherein the latter compares himself to the lost one hundredth sheep when he finds himself alone on the island (Q. p. 95, l. 32–p. 96, l. 20 [p. 116]). He greatly reduces the good man's interpretation of Perceval's dream of the two ladies, one astride a lion and the other, a serpant, leaving out much biblical doctrine and retaining only their significance as the Old and New Law (Q. p. 101, l. 20–p. 104, l. 10 [pp. 121–23]; M. p. 915, ll. 6–25). He completely eliminates a sermon at the beginning of the second Lancelot section on Galahad's predestined role (Q. p. 116, l. 2–p. 117, l. 4 [pp. 134–35]). And he removes a long sermon at the beginning of the Bors section which describes the spiritual purity necessary to achieve the Grail, retaining only a reference to "clennes" and confession. (Q. p. 162, l. 19–p. 164, l. 7 [pp. 176–77]); M. p. 955, ll. 11–14).

Malory even eliminates a reference in the *Queste* to a reported repetition; when Lancelot is with the hermit who interprets his dream, the author writes, "Si l'en remeine en sa chapele et Lancelot li conte toute sa vie einsi *come il l'avoit autre foiz contee*, puis le requiert por Dieu qu'il le conselt" (Q. p. 133, ll. 26–29 [So the hermit led him back to the chapel, where Lancelot told him the burden of his story *as he had told it . . . before*, and after begged him in God's name to counsel him (p. 150; emphasis mine)]. In the *Queste* each repetition of the same thing lends it added significance, and here, even though Lancelot's third confession of his sinful life is not related, the reference to it deepens our sense of the knight's repentence. For Malory, however, Lancelot's actions subsequent to confession are of greater importance, and he thus sees no value in repeating the confession or in retaining a reference to the fact that it was repeated.

The omissions discussed in this section are those that function as *interpretatio* in the *Queste*. Malory has systematically eliminated the allegorical level; the adventures, visions, and dreams remain, but the interpretations of these are either entirely eliminated or radically reduced, retaining only that which is applicable to the moral behavior of man and, more specifically, of those embarked on the quest for the Grail.[4] Malory's treatment of repetition serves the same purpose and has the same effect as his abbreviations of his source's *digressiones*. In both cases he is implicitly following Geoffrey's injunctions to eliminate those devices that contribute to amplification and to narrow the theme. He restricts his story to one time and one level. In so doing, he moves away from Partiality toward Totality, in which the whole appears to be encompassable in the mind's eye.

Thus far we have examined the significance of Malory's omissions from his source; because of our previous analysis of the structure and meaning of the *Queste*, the intention behind Malory's adaptation of that work has begun to emerge. By his consistant efforts to reduce or eliminate *digressio* and *interpretatio*, he confines the quest to the Arthurian world and the actions of men in that world. These emphases emerge as a result of the reductions Malory makes—by default, as it were; however, his intent can be further clarified by an examination of what he adds to his work, material that is different from or absent from his source.

Emphasis

In his instructions on abbreviation, Geoffrey of Vinsauf includes *emphasis*—that is, "saying much in few words." In our analysis of Malory's omissions from his source, we have seen certain emphases emerging. Although his alterations and additions are not extensive, when analyzed in combination with his deletions, they also reveal consistent emphases not found in his source and indicate that Malory approached the Grail story with a clear conception that was not the same as that of the *Queste* author. We have already found that Malory's omissions left a stress on moral behavior with the removal of the *Queste*'s doctrinal allegory. In the *Queste* a knight's ability to penetrate the meanings of events and to do the right thing in accordance with imposed standards is an indication of his spiritual condition and thus his worthiness to achieve the Grail. In Malory a man's worthiness is determined by his actions as judged by conventional Christian morality. Malory's standards of right behavior are thus in accordance with the chivalric code of conduct,[5] whereas the "celestiel" standards of the *Queste* transcend it. Further, Malory emphasizes brotherhood, familial and knightly, in contrast to the *Queste*, in which all earthly ties fade the nearer one approaches perfection. Finally, Malory dwells on the quest of Lancelot more than that of Galahad. The latter, of course, is still the only one to see the secrets of the Grail openly, but Malory's emphasis on earthly morality and human brotherhood causes him to be most concerned with the sincere but flawed quest of the best of all earthly knights. In the following sections these three emphases—morality, brotherhood, and Lancelot—will be discussed by means of an examination of Malory's alterations of and additions to his source.

Morality

Malory's quest is initiated in the same way as is that in the *Queste*: Galahad comes to court and the Grail appears at the Round Table. Except for the alterations in the conception and representation of the Grail noted above, the decision to seek the Grail and the departure of the knights from Arthur's court follow the pattern found in the *Queste*. However, as the knights separate, and their individual quests are described, it becomes clear that their successes or failures are being determined by standards other than those Malory found in his source.

In the *Queste* Melias is punished by God, as the monk explains, for his pride in choosing the left-hand path, that which the inscription said no one should follow unless he be second to none in virtue. Melias is also punished for his covetousness in attempting to take the golden crown he found on that path (Q. p. 44, l. 32–p. 46, l. 12 [pp. 70–71]). In the *Queste* the monk makes clear that when Melias became a knight, he went to confession and purged himself of sin; this so distressed the devil that he threw temptation in Melias's way and Melias fell into the sins of pride and covetousness. This is obviously an unsatisfactory explanation of Melias's adventure to Malory, for he has the monk begin by saying, "And I mervayle . . . how ye durste take uppon you so rych a thynge as the hyghe Order of Knyghthode ys withoute clene confession" (M. p. 886, ll. 9–11). For Malory it is clearly necessary to invent specifically wrong behavior—failure to confess—to account for the punishment God sends Melias.

In the *Queste* the monk also tells Melias that he failed because the inscription referred to "chevalerie celestiel," while Melias understood it as "secular" and thus, relying on his own prowess, fell into pride and presumption. Malory also has the monk say, "the wrytyng on the crosse was a significacyon of hevynly dedys, and of knyghtly dedys in Goddys workys, and no knyghtes dedys in worldly workis" (M. p. 886, ll. 20–22). However, he goes on to state, "And where thou toke the crowne of golde thou ded syn in covetyse and in theffte. All this was no knyghtly dedys" (M. p. 886, ll. 24–26). Although Malory here makes roughly the same division as the *Queste* between "celestiel" and "secular," right action is identified with "knyghtly dedys" or chivalry; to do "knyghtly dedys in Goddys workys" appears to be synonymous with knightly behavior according to the chivalric code. Neither excludes personal prowess, as *chevalerie celestiel* does in the *Queste*. Malory has transformed Melias's sin from an inability to withstand the devil into one of moral misconduct in undertaking knighthood without being confessed and thus falling into sin by covetousness and theft. Malory's addition of theft to Melias's sins is clearly part of the new emphasis he brings to the story of the Grail, for later when a priest explains to Galahad the adventures of the Castle of Maidens, he adds to the sins of the seven brothers, "robbynge and pyllynge the poure comyn peple" (M. p. 889, ll. 18–19). This is not found in Malory's source. He is blackening the crimes of those who are sinners in order that their behavior may be seen as bad by the standards of earthly chivalry.

Similarly, when Gawain kills the same seven brothers whom Galahad defeated, he is chastised by a hermit for reasons other than those given in the French. In the *Queste* Gawain is told that he was received into the order of knighthood "por ce que vos servissiez a nostre criator et deffendissiez Sainte Eglise et rendissiez a Dieu le tresor que il vos bailla a garder, ce est l'ame de vos" (Q. p. 54, ll. 14–16) [in order to serve our Maker, defend Holy Church and render at last to God that treasure which He entrusted to your safekeeping, namely your soul (p. 79)]. In Malory, however, Gawain is told that "whan ye were made first knyght ye sholde have takyn you to knyghtly dedys and vertuous lyvyng" (M. p. 891, ll. 30–32); the hermit goes on to tell Gawain that he has "lyved myschevously many wyntirs" (M. p. 891, l. 33). Whereas in the *Queste* Gawain's sin in killing the seven brothers lies in his prevention of their doing penance and making peace with God (Q. p. 54, ll. 22–26 [p. 79]), in Malory it lies simply in his killing them, immoral enough in itself:

For sertes, had ye nat bene so wycked as ye ar, never had the seven brethirne be slayne by you and youre two felowys: for sir Galahad hymself alone bete hem all seven the day toforne, but hys lyvyng ys such that he shall sle no man lyghtly. (M. p. 892, ll. 2–6)

Furthermore, the hermit here makes a reference to Galahad not found in Malory's source: "And sir Galahad ys a mayde and synned never" (M. p. 891, ll. 33–34). In the *Queste* it is not necessary to account for Galahad's sinlessness; even though it is possible for Galahad to fall into sin, the many references to his spiritual perfection and final achievement of the Grail attest to his Christ-like qualities. However, for Malory, the fact that Galahad is a "mayde" and sinless—he does not lightly kill knights—is evidence that he is in fact worthy of achieving the Grail because he abides by Christian moral conduct.

In the Perceval section another example of such emphasis on moral behavior occurs when Perceval escapes the devil disguised as a beautiful woman. In the *Queste* as soon as Perceval sees the cross inlaid in the hilt of his sword, he comes to his senses ("si li souvint de soi," Q. p. 110, l. 7 [p. 129]). In Malory, however, Perceval also sees the cross "and bethought hym on hys knyghthode and hys promyse made unto the good man tofornehande" (M. p. 918, ll. 31–33). It is thus in Malory Perceval's obligations to others, or moral action, rather than the peril to his own soul, that causes him to escape the devil.

Malory also alters the recluse's interpretation of Lancelot's participation in the tournament between the black and white knights and God's admonition to Lancelot afterwards. In both works the recluse likens the tournament to the quest for the Grail, but in the *Queste*, the black and white knights represent "li chevalier terrien et li chevalier celestiel" (Q. p. 143, ll. 26–27) [earthly knights . . . (and) the knights of heaven (p. 159)], while in Malory they are "erthely kynges and erthely knyghtes" (M. p. 933, l. 23). Malory does make a distinction between the two sides—kings and knights—but neither side is "celestiel." The black knights in the *Queste* are those who are covered with the black wraps of sin, while the white knights are clothed in virginity and chastity; this Malory leaves unchanged, but he adds to the description of the black knights that "the coveryng betokenyth the synnes whereof they be nat confessed" (M. p. 933, ll. 26–27). Thus, not satisfied with the general condition of their being sinners, Malory agains justifies their condemnation by their failure to confess.

More striking, however, is Malory's alteration of Lancelot's sin in helping the black knights. In the *Queste* the knight is told that he helps them because he is a sinner as they are (Q. p. 144, ll. 6–9 [p. 159]). In the spiritual context of the *Queste*, proof of Lancelot's sinfulness lies in his inability to penetrate the meaning of the adventure and thus to know on which side to fight. In Malory, however, Lancelot does not choose the wrong side through spiritual blindness but through pride: "And whan thou saw the synners overcom thou enclyned to that party for bobbaunce and pryde of the worlde, and all that muste be leffte in that queste" (M. p. 933, l. 31–p. 934, l. 1). For Malory Lancelot's sin of vainglory takes place on a level of earthly right and wrong; it is not, as in the French, that Lancelot is unable to perceive the truths behind events, something that is not an action but a state of soul.

Malory also alters the emphasis of a hermit's answer to Gawain's inquiry as to why there are no more adventures. In the *Queste* the hermit's response is an explicit statement of the purpose of the quest and the requirements for success in it (Q. p. 160, l. 33–p. 161, l. 2 [p. 174]). He goes on to detail Gawain's sins that preclude those adventures that are the significances and manifestations of the Grail. The hermit says that Gawain is wrong to think that adventure can now lie in killing knights: "ainz sont des choses esperituex, qui sont graindres et mielz vaillanz assez" (Q. p. 161, ll. 5–6) [they are of a spiritual order, higher in every way and much more worth (p. 174)]. Malory's changes in this passage remove the emphasis from the nature of the quest and place it more directly on what is required to achieve it:

The adventure of the Sankgreall whych be in shewynge now, ye and many other have undertaken the quest of hit and fynde hit not, for hit apperith not to no synners (wherefore mervayle ye nat though ye fayle thereoff and many othir, for ye bene an untrew knyght and a grete murtherar) and to good men signifieth othir thynges than murthir. (M. p. 948, ll. 14–20)

Malory leaves out the hermit's statement that the adventures to happen now concern the nature and manifestations of the Grail, since, as we have seen, for Malory the purpose of the quest is not the unveiling of the meaning of the Grail. However, he also omits it because he is mainly concerned with good knightly conduct. Although the stricture against murder is found in the same place in the *Queste*, Malory adds, "for ye bene an untrew knyght"; an untrue knight in Malory is the counterpart to "desloial pecheor" in the *Queste*. Malory's emphasis is also demonstrated in the changes he makes in the last line of this passage. In the *Queste* the hermit tells Gawain that the adventures of the Grail are of a spiritual order, higher in every way and more valuable than temporal adventures. Malory says that these adventures "to good men signifieth othir thynges than murthir." Thus, although bad moral behavior—such as murder—is as reprehensible in Malory as it is in the *Queste*, to Malory the adventures of the Grail are not necessarily spiritual. Since Malory largely eliminates the allegorical level, the adventures of the Grail take place in the context of literal Christian morality alone.

Brotherhood

Malory's conception of moral behavior can be further clarified by an examination of the emphasis he places on brotherhood, whether familial or knightly. This emphasis is largely absent from his source, for in the *Queste* the closer one approaches perfection, the more earthly ties fall away and are transcended by charity. But Malory places a high value on earthly brotherhood; whether or not a knight displays the qualities brotherhood implies, such as loyalty and fidelity, determines to a large extent Malory's judgment of him. This emphasis is closely related to the emphasis on secular morals, and both are contained in his conception of the quest for the Grail as a story of the struggle of earthly men to be worthy Christian knights. Malory's emphasis on brotherhood is demonstrated by short but frequent additions to his source that, taken together, significantly alter the intent of the work.

Malory consistently stresses the bond among the knights of the Round Table; he has an obvious admiration for earthly chivalry as an ideal, and this ideal is for him embodied in the knights of Arthur's court. The behavior of knights in the light of ideal earthly chivalry informs the narrative in Malory's work, just as do the knights' responses in the *Queste* to the *celestiel* standards set by the presence of the Grail. Foremost among the qualities required in Malory's chivalry is brotherhood among knights. Thus, it follows that Malory's first addition emphasizing brotherhood occurs during the initial appearance of the Grail at Arthur's court. As in the *Queste*, the Grail's appearance is accompanied by thunder, a sunbeam, sweet fragrances, choice food; and all those present are struck dumb. In Malory, however, the Grail affects the knights' perceptions of each other: "Than began every knyght to beholde other, and eyther saw other, by their semynge, fayrer than ever they were before" (M. p. 865, ll. 21–23). This statement could have no place in the *Queste*, where the appearance of the Grail summons the knights to prove their worthiness on a level beyond all that which they have known and where earthly attachments must give way to spiritual demands. Malory's addition links the initial appearance of the Grail to the idea of brotherhood.

That brotherhood among men is an ideal in Malory is demonstrated in numerous of his other alterations and additions. For example, in response to Perceval's request to be allowed to leave the barren island, Malory has the good man refer to knighthood rather than the grace of God, as in the *Queste*. In the latter, the good man tells Perceval that he will get away in God's good time, for God alone can determine whether Perceval has proven himself His faithful servant. Perceval must of course be a "loiax chevaliers" (Q. p. 99, l. 33) [true knight (p.

120)], but this is to be understood in the sense of celestial chivalry and is thus corollary to the injunctions to be God's servant. Malory leaves out most of the good man's response, retaining only what is required of Perceval according to knightly brotherhood:

Doute ye nat . . . and ye be so trew a knyght as the Order of Shevalry requyrith, and of herte as ye ought to be, ye shold nat doute that none enemy shold slay you. (M. p. 914, ll. 32–35)

The brotherhood of chivalry in Malory provides adequate standards for right action, whereas in the *Queste* secular standards must be transcended.

That the values of chivalry can be appealed to for such right action in Malory's world is evident in the Bors section, when Bors sees the maiden being carried off by the knight intent on ravishing her. In the *Queste* she asks Bors to help her by the faith he owes to God (Q. p. 175, ll. 22–25 [p. 188]). In Malory she also asks Bors's help in the name of God, but Malory adds, "and for the feythe ye owe to the hyghe Ordre of Knyghthode, and for kynge Arthures sake, which I suppose made the knyght" (M. p. 961, ll. 8–11). Since for Malory ideal earthly chivalry is the standard against which men are measured, it is within this brotherhood of knights Arthur has brought into being that Malory sees the potential for worthiness to achieve the Grail.

Since the brotherhood was created for and dedicated to a noble yet secular ideal, the worst sin is for brother to turn against brother. The hermit interprets Gawain's dream of the bulls at the hayrack to refer to those knights of the Round Table who were patient and humble until their sins made them fail in the Grail quest; Malory retains only those features specifically related to the fate of this brotherhood. Although far shorter than the *Queste*, his version does retain a description of the Round Table in times past: "therefore was the Rounde Table founden, and the shevalry hath ben at all tymes so hyghe by

the fraternité which was there that she myght nat be overcom"
(M. p. 946, ll. 9–11). Then when the bulls set out for new
pasture—that is, the knights set out on the quest for the
Grail—sin hindered their progress. In the *Queste* the hermit
expostulates at length upon the failure of the Round Table
knights—except for Galahad, Perceval, and Bors—as due to
"luxure" and "orgueil" (Q. p. 156, ll. 14–15) ["lechery" and
"pride" (p. 170)]. In fact, some of the knights on the quest are
so steeped in sin that they will kill other knights: "cil qui
revendront seront si essorbé de pechié que li un avront ocis les
autres" (Q. p. 157, ll. 15–17) [those who return will be so
blinded with sin that some will have killed their fellows (p.
171)]. Malory eliminates almost all of the sermon, blaming the
knights' failures only on lack of "good vertues or workes" (M.
p. 946, ll. 19–20); and he concludes:

And therefore they turned into waste contreyes: that signifieth dethe,
for there shall dye many off them. For everych of them shall sle othir
for synne. (M. p. 946, ll. 33–35)

For Malory murder is a sin against chivalric brotherhood; the
action, regardless of the lack of spiritual understanding underlying it, is for him sufficient to cause failure in the quest for the
Grail. "Luxure" and "orgueil" are irrelevent; whereas murder
followed lust and pride in the *Queste*, Malory makes it a primary sin.

The most striking example of Malory's emphasis on brother-
hood occurs in the context of Gawain's killing of Uwayne, an-
other knight of the Round Table. In both the *Queste* and Malory,
Gawain mortally wounds Uwayne (Yvain) and takes him to an
abbey, each knight still not recognizing the other. The *Queste*
Gawain asks the wounded knight who he is; still not knowing
Gawain, Yvain tells him, adding his forgiveness, since Yvain
believes his death must have come about through the will of
God or his own sin (Q. p. 153, ll. 23–29 [p. 168]). In Malory,
Uwayne does know Gawain, and his response is far harsher:

Sir . . . I am of kynge Arthures courte, and was a felow of the Rounde Table, and we were sworne togydir. And now, sir Gawayne, thou hast slayne me. And my name ys sir Uwayne le Avoutres, that somtyme was sone unto kynge Uryen, and I was in the queste of the Sankgreall. And now forgyff the God, for hit shall be ever rehersed that the tone sworne brother hath slayne the other. (M. p. 944, l. 31–p. 945, l. 4)

Malory then follows his source in having Uwayne say that his death could not have come from a better—"worshipfuller"— man's hand. In the *Queste* Yvain then asks Gawain to tell his companions to pray that God may have mercy on his soul (Q. p. 153, l. 33–p. 154, l. 7 [p. 168]). In Malory, however, he asks to be remembered for the sake of brotherhood:

But whan ye com to the courte recommaunde me unto my lorde Arthur, and to all them that be leffte on lyve. And for olde brothirhode thynke on me. (M. p. 945, ll. 9–11)

The significance of this alteration is paradigmatic of the principle guiding Malory's adaptation throughout the *Queste* material. Knightly brotherhood is potentially and ideally noble, moral, and good. Uwayne recalls that he and Gawain were "sworne togydir" and is happy that if he must die, it can be at the hand of such a worshipful man. Yet the ominous ring of the phrase, not in Malory's source, that "hit shall be ever rehersed that the tone sworne brother hath slayne the other" indicates that it is by these standards, the standards of the chivalric code and earthly Christian knighthood, that most of the knights are judged. Malory's source is very clear about Gawain's failure in the quest, but in that work it is the knight's incorrigible spiritual blindness, his inability to see beyond the literal meaning of events to their true significance, that causes his failure. In Malory killing his sworn brother makes Gawain fail on the literal level; he does wrong in this world, and by Malory's standards that is bad enough. The value placed on knightly brotherhood is poignantly expressed in Malory's addition to Uwayne's last words to Gawain: "And for olde brothirhode thynke on me."

Besides knightly brotherhood, Malory also emphasizes familial brotherhood to an extent not found in his source. Most of his additions of this kind stress the bonds between brothers or cousins who are also fellow knights; however, because Malory is careful to point out the familial relationships among them and obviously considers these important, they will be discussed separately below. Further, since many of Malory's changes emphasizing the familial bonds involve Lancelot, these will be examined in the next section focusing on that knight.

Near the beginning of the work, Galahad, barely arrived at court and having claimed his seat at the Round Table, succeeds in drawing the mysterious sword from the stone. This is one of the signs indicating that the quest for the Grail is to begin. In the *Queste* after gaining the sword, Galahad merely says that he now better equipped than he was before and lacks only a shield (Q. p. 12, ll. 18–19 [p. 41]). However, Malory has Galahad describe the origin of the sword, an origin not mentioned in the *Queste*:

Now have I the swerde that somtyme was the good knyghtes Balyns le Saveaige, and he was a passynge good knyght of hys hondys; and with thys swerde he slew hys brothir Balan, and that was grete pité, for he was a good knyght. And eythir slew othir thorow a dolerous stroke that Balyn gaff unto kynge Pelles, the whych ys nat yett hole, nor naught shall be tyll that I hele hym. (M. p. 863, ll. 3–9)

Although referring back to the story of Balin, this passage plays a significant role within the *Sankgreal* itself.[6] The addition occurs shortly before the appearance at Arthur's court of the Grail, which causes the knights to see each other "fayrer than ever they were before" (M. p. 865, l. 23). The juxtaposition of these passages introduces the principles which inform the narrative. Galahad possesses the sword that was the agent of an unbrotherly act, Balin's murder of his brother Balan; his coming to court has initiated the quest for the Grail, in which men will succeed or fail according to the standards of Arthurian chivalry. The first appearance of the Grail reveals the sense of fellowship that is for Malory an integral part of true chivalry.

Thus, the quest is an attempt on the part of the knights to live up to the chivalric ideal and thereby undo Balin's "dolerous stroke." Only by doing so can they achieve the Grail.

Numerous short references to familial brotherhood in Malory enhance his emphasis on fidelity in brotherhood as necessary for those who are worthy Christians. In the *Queste* a monk explains to Galahad the significance of the adventure of the tomb and includes these words: "Car li filz n'amoit le pere ne li peres l'enfant (Q. p. 37, l. 33–p. 38, l. 1) [sons loved not their fathers nor fathers their sons (p. 63)]. In Malory the intepretation has disappeared, leaving four short sentences that include the following: "For there was suche wrecchydnesse that the fadir loved nat the sonne, nother the sonne loved nat the fadir" (M. p. 882, ll. 31–33). What was in the *Queste* an example among many of the wickedness that made Christ's coming necessary has become in Malory the only example adduced. In the Perceval section there is a similar reference to familial treachery that Malory retains:

And as the tale tellith, he was at that tyme, one of the men of the worlde whych moste beleved in oure Lorde Jesu Cryste, for in tho dayes there was but fewe folkes at that tyme that beleved perfitely; for in tho dayes the sonne spared not the fadir no more than a straunger. (M. p. 913, ll. 5–9)

This is a fairly close rendering of the French (Q. p. 95, ll. 14–22 [p. 115–16], except that in the *Queste* this behavior is attributed only to the Welsh. The significance of the passage for Malory lies in the fact that although he eliminated much of the material surrounding it in his source, such as Perceval's long prayer, he did include this further example of unbrotherly behavior.

The Bors section also contains examples of emphasis on brotherhood. Upon Bors's agreeing to fight Priadan le Noir for the lady of the castle, that lady and her wicked sister meet on the field of battle. In the *Queste* version of the episode, the lady of the castle accuses her sister of seizing her inheritance (Q. p. 172, ll. 30–33 [p. 185]). In Malory she says, "Madam, ye have done grete wronge to beryve me my landis that kyng Anyauss gaff me, and full lothe I am there sholde be ony batayle" (M. p. 959, ll. 9–11). Her reluctance to see a battle between Bors and her sister's champion is found nowhere in the *Queste*; the younger sister's reservations about waging war with her own sister make her, in Malory's eyes, worthy of Bors's defense. Later when Bors is led by the false priest to the castle of the maiden who threatens to kill herself for his love, he is warmly welcomed by all those present, and the *Queste* adds this made him partly forget his grief (Q. p. 180, ll. 12–13 [p. 192]). This grief is for Bors's brother Lionel, supposedly dead, although Lionel is not named there. In Malory, however, he is:

So they made hym such chere that he had forgotyn hys sorrow and anguysshe and only sette his herte in these delytes and deyntees, and tooke no thought more for his brother sir Lyonell neyther of sir Launcelot du Lake, his cosyn. (M. p. 964, ll. 21–25)

For Malory a measure of the strength of the temptation offered Bors by the devil is that it makes the knight forget even brother and cousin. When Bors ultimately overcomes, his victory is therefore the more remarkable.

Malory's emphasis on brotherhood is also evident when Lionel tries to kill Bors. In both works Bors is innocent, since God had shown him in a dream that he must save a maiden (the lily), rather than Lionel (the rotten wood). Near the conclusion of the episode, however, when all of Bors's pleas to Lionel have been to no avail, he prays to God. In the *Queste* he also asks that his self-defense not be held against him (Q. p. 193, ll. 4–6 [p. 204]). Malory's passage is longer, and Bors addresses his prayer first to Lionel:

Well . . . fayre brother, God knowith myne entente, for ye have done full evyll thys day to sle an holy pryste which never trespasced. Also ye have slayne a jantill knyght, and one of oure felowis. And well wote ye that I am nat aferde of you gretely, but I drede the wratthe of God; and thys ys an *unkyndely* werre. Therefore God shew His myracle uppon us bothe, and God have mercy uppon me, thoughe I defende my lyff ayenst my brothir. (M. p. 973, ll. 23–31; emphasis mine)

Malory's Bors gives reasons for defending himself: Lionel's unbrotherly behavior towards another knight and the murder of a priest. By listing Lionel's crimes, Malory's Bors shows more reluctance to fight Lionel than he does in the *Queste*. Bors's concern in Malory is not only that God forgive him but also that Lionel understand that Bors does not wish to fight him. In the *Queste* after God has stopped the fight, Bors repeats that Lionel did wrong in committing murder (Q. p. 193, ll. 23–25 [p. 205]). In Malory Bors asks Lionel's forgiveness as his brother, and Lionel grants it (M. p. 974, ll. 14–17). With that, Bors leaves, no longer reproaching Lionel. This example of brotherly reconciliation has no place in the *Queste*, for in that work God's intervention calls Bors to higher duties, and from that moment he has scarcely a thought to spare for his brother. For Malory Bors's fraternal gestures suggest his worthiness for the adventures of the Grail.

Malory's emphasis on brotherhood is indeed an integral part of his conception of the quest for the Grail; those who fail do not do so on the level of spiritual perfection but on the level of "knyghtly dedys and vertuous lyvyng" (M. p. 891, ll. 31–32). Arthur knows from the beginning that many will fail in the quest; therefore, he calls for a tournament, so that he may see them all together one more time. In the *Queste* Arthur merely announces that the quest for the Grail is to begin; since he knows he will never see his knights all assembled again, he proposes so splendid a tournament that after their deaths people will continue to speak of it (Q. p. 13, ll. 21–26 [p. 42]). Malory's Arthur says essentially the same thing, but his words lay more stress on the brotherhood of the Round Table knights:

Now, . . . I am sure at this quest of the Sankegreall shall all ye of the Rownde Table departe, and nevyr shall I se you agayne holé togydirs, therefore ones shall I se you togydir in the medow, all holé togydirs! Therefore I wol se you all holé togydir in the medow of Camelot, to juste and to turney, that aftir youre dethe men may speke of hit that such good knyghtes were here, such a day, holé togydirs (M. p. 864, ll. 5–12)

The remarkable repetition of "holé togydirs," completely foreign to Malory's source, underscores what is for Malory the beauty and strength of this fellowship as well as the tragedy that not all of its members can measure up to the ideals it embodies.

Lancelot

At the center of Malory's concern for morality is brotherhood, and at the center of the brotherhood of knights stands Lancelot, flawed exemplar of the best that secular knighthood has to offer. Since Malory's interest lies in the struggles of men to become worthy of achieving the Grail, he concentrates on Lancelot, whose efforts to rise above sin link him to the majority of mankind, rather than on Galahad, who, as Perceval's aunt tells Perceval, "worchith all by myracle"[7] (M. p. 906, l. 13). Lancelot incorporates Malory's emphases on morality and loyal brotherhood as the knight's role in the quest expands in comparison to the *Queste*. It is through an examination of Malory's alterations in Lancelot's character and development that the purpose behind his adaptation can be clearly discerned.

Malory radically alters Lancelot's faults as he finds them in the *Queste*, where Lancelot was condemned to failure—or at best only a partial success—by his spiritual blindness, his inability to see the truth behind events. There in spite of sincere efforts, Lancelot's sinful past weighs him down and makes it impossible for him ever to give up completely responding to situations as he had before the arrival of the Grail. In Malory Lancelot's faults have far more to do with right action than with spiritual insight, and he is not so harshly condemned as he is in the *Queste*.[8] To a large extent, Malory has transformed Lancelot's experience in the quest from one of failure to one of almost complete success.

From the beginning of the *Sankgreal*, Lancelot's relationship to Galahad is stressed by additions to the *Queste* which enhance his role. Both works begin with Lancelot's knighting of Galahad and Galahad's subsequent arrival at Arthur's court. In the *Queste* Bors and Lionel suggest to Lancelot that Galahad is his son, but Lancelot refuses to respond (Q. p. 3, l. 25–p. 4, l. 2 [p. 33]; p. 9, ll. 18–31 [pp. 38–39]). Malory omits these suggestions by Bors and Lionel, although he does acknowledge that Lancelot recognizes Galahad as his son (M. p. 861, ll. 13–14). The alteration increases Lancelot's insight and perspicacity as well as enhancing his role by association with Galahad, the knight who will achieve the Grail. In the *Queste* Guinevere explains Galahad's ancestry to one of her ladies by simply stating that he descends from noble knights on both sides (Q. p. 14, l. 33–p. 15, l. 2 [p. 43]). Malory expands upon her explanation:

Ye, forsothe, . . . for he ys of all partyes comyn of the beste knyghtes of the worlde and of the hyghest lynage: for sir Launcelot ys com but of the eyghth degré frome oure Lorde Jesu Cryst, and thys sir Galahad ys the nyneth degré from oure Lorde Jesu Cryst. Therefore I dare sey they be the grettist jantillmen of the worlde. (M. p. 865, ll. 7–12)

By lauding Lancelot as "but of the eyghth degré" from Christ, Malory brings him into the glory of Galahad.

Nonetheless, it is true that in both works Galahad's coming alters his father's reputation. After Galahad draws the sword from the stone, Malory follows his source in having a maiden ride up announcing to Lancelot that henceforth he can no longer think of himself as the best knight of the world. In the *Queste*, Lancelot meekly acquiesces in the judgment (Q. p. 12, l. 27–p. 13, l. 8 [pp. 41–42]); however, Malory expands his answer: "As towchyng unto that . . . I know well I was never none of the beste" (M. p. 863, ll. 28–29). Such modesty is lacking in the *Queste*. Malory then has the maiden summarize his own attitude toward Lancelot: "Yes, . . . that were ye, and ar yet, of ony synfull man of the worlde" (M. p. 863, ll. 30–31). This is wholly Malory's invention and adumbrates his treatment of Lancelot throughout his *Sankgreal*. Lancelot is the best of all secular knights, and that is sufficient for Malory to let him come closer to achieving the Grail than he does in the *Queste*. Yet he is also sinful, and so his achievement cannot be as complete as Galahad's.

The first major section devoted to Lancelot contains the same episodes as the *Queste* but with a different emphasis. Malory includes the episode in which Lancelot lies in a trance, unable to move when the Grail comes into his presence. However, Malory adds that "aftir that many men seyde hym shame, but he toke repentaunce aftir that" (M. p. 895, ll. 1–2). This is an obvious effort to resurrect Lancelot's reputation by indicating that he will improve. The statement does not occur in the *Queste*, for there it is his slow, steady attempt to become worthy that is instructive, and to indicate so early that he succeeds would be to undercut the salutory emphasis on humiliation and repentance. For Malory it is more instructive to reveal at the outset that Lancelot will overcome and become worthy, even if he can never completely achieve the Grail.

More remarkable, however, are the changes Malory makes in Lancelot's lamentations when he realizes he has failed in this adventure and also in his confession to the hermit. In the *Queste* after God calls him harder than stone, more bitter than wood, and more barren than the fig tree, he curses the day he was born because he has failed to pierce the secret of the Grail, and he vows to discover the meaning of the words spoken to him (Q. p. 61, ll. 21–28 [p. 85]). Malory significantly alters his source: "And so departed sore wepynge and cursed the tyme that he was borne, for than he demed never to have worship more. For tho wordis wente to hys herte, tylle that he knew wherefore he was called so" (M. p. 895, ll. 30–33). Rather than lamenting his failure to penetrate the mysteries of the Grail, Malory's Lancelot despairs of ever having honor again; however, since Malory's Grail is not shrouded in secrecy like that of the *Queste* but is rather a comprehensible object to be attained by worthy men, the knight's lament is appropriate. He laments his failure to be worthy of achieving the Grail, for as Bors says, "he shall have much erthly worship that may bryng hit to an ende" (M. p. 955, ll. 9–10). Lancelot thus experiences in Malory a failure in chivalry, not in spiritual understanding. This is in keeping with Malory's emphasis on chivalric behavior. Another change in this passage reinforces his general enhancement of Lancelot. In the *Queste* Lancelot is struck by

ryght other wronge. And never dud I batayle all only for Goddis sake, but for to wynne worship and to cause me the bettir to be beloved, and litill or nought I thanked never God of hit. (M. p. 897, ll. 17–22)

In the *Queste* Lancelot also confesses his love for Guinevere and states that all his feats of prowess have been done for her sake alone; he does not, however, make the distinction that Malory's Lancelot does between right and wrong (Q. p. 66, ll. 8–18 [p. 89]). From the point of view of the author of the *Queste*, anything Lancelot did for Guinevere was *luxure* and therefore wrong. This love must also be condemned because it is characteristic of secular chivalry, not the "chevalerie celestielle" of the quest for the Grail. However, for Malory a knight is tested and must prove himself according to the guidelines set by ideal secular chivalry and thus moral action; hence, it matters very much whether Lancelot's actions in Guinevere's behalf are right or wrong.[9] Because this moral distinction is Malory's invention and not found in his source, it is clear that he did not find sufficient justification in the *Queste* for Lancelot's condemnation and so added what was for him a real flaw in accordance with his own conception of worthiness in the quest.

Along with altering the character of Lancelot's sin in this section, Malory continues to present him in a more positive light than does the *Queste*. Lancelot's condemnation is not so harsh nor is his humiliation so great as in the French. There the voice of God asks how he dares come before the Holy Grail and befoul the place by his presence (Q. p. 61, ll. 18–20 [p. 85]). In Malory he is simply told, "Therefore go thou from hens, and withdraw the from thys holy places!" (M. p. 895, ll. 27–28). In the *Queste* when daylight breaks after his night of lamentations, the song of the birds casts Lancelot into further despair because he remembers his former joy and is now wretched in the knowledge of God's anger (Q. p. 62, ll. 8–19 [p. 86]). In Malory he also sorrows through the night, but at daybreak he "harde the fowlys synge; than somwhat he was comforted" (M. p. 896, ll. 10–11). For Malory it seems reasonable that things associated with Lancelot's formerly knightly life should comfort him, since there is no longer a sharp division between secular chivalry and the quest for the Grail as set forth in the French. Later in the *Queste*, after Lancelot has promised the hermit to forswear Guinevere, the hermit adjures him to live in true repentance and explains that by this means God will again count him as one of His own (Q. p. 66, l. 23–p. 67, l. 4 [p. 90]). In Malory, however, the hermit says, "Sir, loke that your harte and youre mowth accorde . . . and I shall ensure you ye shall have the more worship than ever ye had" (M. p. 897, ll. 29–31). The proper goal of knights in the *Queste* is definitely not to "have the more worship"; however, Malory's alteration is again consistent with his emphasis on ideal chivalry as a worthy goal. [10]

Lancelot's humiliation is also lessened in this section by the abbreviation of the hermit's sermons. In the *Queste* previous to Lancelot's confession, a hermit discourses at length on the return the knight owes God for having bestowed on him so many talents and includes an account of the Parable of the Talents (Q. p. 63, l. 13–p. 64, l. 25 [pp. 87–88]). Malory eliminates the parable and concentrates on Lancelot's gifts from God, among which is "worldly worship," not mentioned in the *Queste* (M. p. 896, l. 29–p. 897, l. 7). Similarly, in the *Queste* Lancelot's request to have the hermit explain why he was called harder than stone, more bitter than wood, and more barren than a fig tree is followed by a lengthy disquisition on his faults (Q. p. 67, l. 25–p. 70, l. 25 [pp. 90–93]). The hermit does preface his sermon by saying that it is no wonder if more marvelous things are said to Lancelot than to other knights, since he has always been the most marvelous of knights; yet the effect of this statement is quite different from that with which the hermit introduces his sermon in Malory: "Have ye no mervayle . . . thereoff, for hit semyth well God lovith you" (M. p. 897, ll. 35–36). The implication of this remark in the *Queste* is that Lancelot has always been the best knight and thus owes God the most gratitude; therefore, it is not surprising that God singled him out for more severe censure. Malory reinterprets the incident to mean that since God troubled himself to speak to Lancelot at all, "hit semyth well God lovith you." Thus, the hermit's recriminations are not so harsh as in the *Queste*. And since they occupy far less space in the narrative, their emphasis is further diminished.

Malory's alterations in the second Lancelot section further emphasize him as the paragon of earthly chivalry. At the beginning of this section in the *Queste*, the hermit with whom Lancelot remains at the end of the first section delivers a sermon which Malory eliminates. The reasons for this are obvious: the hermit in the *Queste* speaks primarily of the perfection of Galahad and of the nature of the quest in a manner not suited to Malory's conception of it (Q. p. 116, l. 2–p. 117, l. 4 [pp. 134–35]). For example, the hermit says, "Car vos savez bien que ceste Queste est emprise por savoir aucune chose des merveilles dou Saint Graal" (Q. p. 116, ll. 7–9) [You are aware that this quest was undertaken to glean some knowledge of the mysteries of the Holy Grail (p. 134)]. For Malory the quest is not undertaken to gain knowledge of the mysteries of the Grail, so he eliminates the statement. The hermit also tells Lancelot that "cist servises ou vos estes entrez n'apartient de riens as terrianes choses, mes as celestiex" (Q. p. 116, ll. 25–27) [this service in which you are entered does not pertain in any way to the things of earth, but of heaven (p. 134)], and adds that he must not be of such weak faith to presume to "plus fere por sa chevalerie que par la grace de Nostre Seignor" (Q. p. 117, ll. 1–2) [achieve more by his prowess than by the grace of Our Lord (p. 135)]. Since Malory sees much to be praised in doing good works of chivalry and views the quest as primarily concerned with *terrianes choses*, the *Queste*'s emphasis at that point must have seemed excessive.

Malory also eliminates the episode of the berating squire (Q. p. 117, l. 17–p. 118, l. 28 [pp. 135–36]). In the French Lancelot meets a squire who reproaches him for his past misdeeds and in fact heaps vilification on him. He says Lancelot is faithless both as a Christian and as a knight, and goes so far as to assert that "mout poez avoir grant duel, qui soliez estre tenuz au meillor chevalier dou monde, or estes tenuz au plus mauvés et au plus desloial!" (Q. p. 118, ll. 2–4) [you have good cause to grieve, you who once were held to be the best knight in the world and now are shown the worst and most disloyal! (p. 136)]. He also insults Guinevere by saying that she never really loved Lancelot because she has brought him to his present state. In the *Queste* Lancelot's progress is demonstrated by his ability to remain silent in the face of such criticism, which touches even his lady; earthly chivalry would surely have demanded vengeance. However, Malory does not consider Lancelot the worst and most disloyal knight; he considers him to be the most chivalrous one, although a sinner. He therefore does not subject him to the humiliation deemed necessary by the author of the *Queste*. Nor does Malory condemn Lancelot's love for Guinevere so harshly as the author of his source. In his earlier confession Lancelot said that he loved a queen unmeasurably and because of it participated in wrong battles; this for Malory is his sin, not his love for Guinevere in itself. He therefore does not follow the author of the *Queste* in his wholesale condemnation of Guinevere, suppressing the issue entirely by excising the whole episode. [11]

Malory's enhancement of Lancelot's role continues in the next incident, where the devil appears to Lancelot and a monk. In the *Queste* Lancelot cannot see the devil; in Malory he can. In the former after the devil's explanation and disappearance, Lancelot asks the hermit:

Sire, . . . qui fu cil qui tant a parlé a vos? Son cors ne poï je veoir, mes sa parole oï je bien, qui est si laide et si espoantable qu'il n'est nus qui poor n'en deust avoir.'' (Q. p. 122, ll. 20–22)

[Sir, . . . who was it that spoke to you at such length? I could not see him, but I heard his voice, which is grisly and dreadful enough to strike fear into any heart (p. 140)].

Lancelot's blindness signals his lack of spiritual insight and leads to the hermit's pronouncement that he would no more be able to see the Grail were it to appear than a blind man would be able to see a bright sword (Q. p. 123, ll. 5–8 [p. 140]). The hermit then lists the virtues that inhered in Lancelot until he was overcome by lust and thus blinded (Q. p. 123, l. 20–p. 126, l. 11 [pp. 141–43]), stating that if he had kept the virtues

God gave him, Lancelot would not have lain blind in the presence of his Lord but would have seen Him face to face (Q. p. 126, ll. 32–33 [p. 144]). Thus, the *Queste* draws an elaborate analogy between Lancelot's literal inability to see the devil and his spiritual inability to see the Grail, the ultimate goal of the quest. However, since Malory's emphasis is on Lancelot's flawed greatness, rather than his spiritual failings, he eliminates the elaboration on blindness and in fact begins the episode by saying, "And with that *they* saw the fyende in an hydeous fygure, that there was no man so hardé-herted in the worlde but he sholde a bene aferde" (M. p. 925, ll. 20–22; emphasis mine). Because Lancelot can see the devil in Malory, the episode serves as an example of the adventures granted to him, rather than as a demonstration of his lack of understanding.

Of course, when Lancelot later tells the hermit he is seeking the Grail, the hermit's response is similar to that in the *Queste*: "Well . . . seke ye hit ye may well, but thoughe hit were here ye shall have no power to se hit, no more than a blynde man that sholde se a bryght swerde" (M. p. 927, ll. 12–14). But because Malory has left out the many references to Lancelot's blindness, the statement is an isolated criticism rather than another element in a complex metaphorical delineation of sin. Malory himself seems to feel the statement is stark enough to require some explanation, for he has the hermit add, "And that ys longe on youre synne, and ellys ye were more abeler than ony man lyvynge" (M. p. 927, ll. 14–16). Not only does this addition provide a context for the reference to blindness; it also recalls anew Lancelot's relative knightly valor.

Malory's emphasis on Lancelot is also demonstrated in the account of his dream of his lineage. In both the *Queste* and in Malory, Lancelot dreams he sees God in the company of seven kings and two knights who ask Him to render unto each his due (Q. p. 130, l. 29–p. 131, l. 28 [pp. 147–48]); M. p. 928, l. 19–p. 929, l. 2). In both works Lancelot is singled out for his sinfulness. In the *Queste* the figure representing Lancelot in the dream flees the company, grieving and praying for mercy. God then turns to Galahad, transforms him into a lion with wings, and says to him, "Biax filz, or puez aler par tot le monde et voler sus tote chevalerie" (Q. p. 131, ll. 22–23) [Beloved son, now canst thou range over all the world and soar above the ranks of chivalry (p. 148)]. Galahad then flies up to heaven, which opens to receive him. This entire section concerning Galahad is eliminated in Malory; instead, he ends the episode with God's words to Lancelot.

Similarly, Malory changes the character of the hermit's interpretation of this dream and adapts what he finds in his source, partly by reducing greatly this interpretation (Q. p. 134, l. 7–p. 138, l. 8 [pp. 150–54]; M. p. 929, l. 31–p. 930, l. 18). Malory eliminates the account of Mordrain's dream, which is in the *Queste* the means whereby the hermit interprets Lancelot's dream. There Mordrain's dream of a lineage to follow and Lancelot's dream of a past lineage are combined by the hermit, permitting an interpenetration of historical epochs. However, Malory narrows and concentrates events to one time and one level, exchanging allegorical and figural significance for directness and immediacy. Where the French presents Lancelot as part of a glorious lineage leading to Galahad, Malory makes him the central figure to which all else refers. Moreover, although Malory leaves out much of what the hermit says in praise of Galahad,[12] what he does include, rather than throwing shame on Lancelot, tends rather to exonerate him: "And the last was the ninth knyght, he was signyfyed to a lyon, for he sholde passe all maner of erthely knyghtes: that ys sir Galahad whych thou gate on kynge Pelles doughter" (M. p. 930, ll. 11–14). Here Lancelot's fatherhood is stressed to an extent not found in the *Queste*. Finally, Malory adds to the hermit's interpretation the passage cited earlier, again not present in his source and which epitomizes his adaptation of Lancelot's character:

And thou ought to thanke God more than ony othir man lyvyng, for of a synner erthely thou hast no pere as in knyghthode nother never shall have. But lytyll thanke hast thou yevyn to God for all the grete vertuys that God hath lente the. (M. p. 930, ll. 14–18)

Above, the hermit had said that Galahad would "passe all maner of erthely knyghts"; Lancelot, however, has not now nor ever shall have a peer in chivalry "of a synner erthely." Galahad does not draw Malory's interest; perfect and distinct, Galahad soars above earthly men. However, through Lancelot, earthly sinner but the best that human chivalry has to offer, Malory can present the possibilities for worthiness within ideal—yet secular—knightly conduct. Lancelot has faults— he has fought the wrong battles and has forgotten to thank God—but his sincere attempts to repent and overcome these faults occupy Malory more than do the knight's failings.

That Lancelot has not yet understood all the hermits have told him is clear in the tournament between the black and white knights. In the *Queste* Lancelot helps the black knights, the wrong side, because he still lacks spiritual insight. As the anchoress explains, the black knights were the sinners, the white knights righteous men; Lancelot proved his sinfulness by joining the former (Q. p. 144, ll. 6–9 [p. 159]). In Malory, however, Lancelot goes to help the black knights, the weaker side, "in incresyng of his shevalry" (M. p. 931, l. 25). He is again undertaking a wrong battle to prove his valour. The anchoress explains his sin to him: "And whan thou saw the synners overcom thou enclyned to that party for bobbaunce and pryde of the worlde" (M. p. 933, ll. 31–32). Thus, it is not Lancelot's inability to see the truth behind events that is condemned in Malory but his pride. These two sins are of a different order, for in the *Queste* Lancelot is required to rise above all that secular chivalry demands and see earthly life with new spiritual vision, whereas in Malory he is required to fulfill the demands of ideal chivalry, which means foregoing pride in his own abilities and instead using them to do good. The anchoress concludes her interpretation of the tournament by recognizing, as did previous hermits, Lancelot's great potential for worthy behavior:

Now have I warned the of thy vayneglory and of thy pryde, that thou haste many tyme arred ayenste thy Maker. Beware of everlastynge payne, for of all erthly knyghtes I have most pité of the, for I know well thou haste nat thy pere of ony erthly synfull man. (M. p. 934, ll. 19–23)

In Malory Lancelot's prowess is a virtue if used rightly and without vainglory, whereas in the *Queste* he is constantly adjured by hermits to rely only on God and not to trust his own prowess. This distinction is clearly demonstrated in the episode by the River Marcoise. In the *Queste* Lancelot arrives at the river's edge only to have a mysterious knight ride up and kill his horse. He finds himself completely hemmed in and helpless, with the river before him, cliffs to either side, and a forest behind. Lancelot accepts the confinement and passively waits for God to deliver him; he is for the first time totally surrendering his will to God's (Q. p. 146, ll. 20–21 [p. 161]).[13] Malory radically transforms this episode. Lancelot arrives at the river, "And thorow the watir he muste nedis passe, the whych was hedyous. And than in the name of God he toke hit with good herte" (M. p. 934, ll. 27–29). Lancelot trusts God to help him cross the river, thereby demonstrating his faith; and he does cross. This is also a valorous action, which Malory believes further demonstrates Lancelot's worthiness. Malory's standards do not require passive acceptance but rather deeds of prowess in the name of God. In Malory Lancelot's horse is killed only after he has already crossed the river, and Lancelot then "toke hys helme and hys shylde, and thanked God of hys adventure" (M. p. 935, ll. 3–4). Thus, although Malory removed the spiritual significance of this episode, he substituted meaning of his own. Just as at this point in the *Queste*, Lancelot demonstrates progress on the road to becoming worthy, he does so in Malory also; previously many hermits have criticized Lancelot for his failure to thank God for his many gifts, but here he "thanked God of hys adventure."

In the Gawain section following Lancelot's adventures, Malory makes additions to his source, specifically delineating Lancelot's character. Gawain, in a moment of perception remarkable for him, says, "And if one thynge were nat in sir Launcelot he had none felow of an erthely man; but he ys as we be but if he take the more payne uppon hym" (M. p. 941, ll.

20–22). That Lancelot has been trying to "take the more payne uppon hym" is evident from the change Malory makes in Lancelot's acceptance of the hair shirt the hermit gives him to wear as penance for his sins. In the *Queste* Lancelot is driven so far from worldly considerations that he does not feel the pricking of the hair and in fact finds pleasure in wearing it (Q. p. 139, ll. 15–22 [p. 155]). Malory changes this to emphasize Lancelot's struggle to bear the shirt: "And so leyde hem to reste, and the heyre prycked faste sir Launcelot's skynne and greved him sore, but he toke hyt mekely and suffirde the payne" (M. p. 931, ll. 7–10). Malory makes Lancelot's victory more difficult than it is in the *Queste* yet also more chivalric than spiritual. Nonetheless, in spite of the pain Lancelot takes upon himself, he is still, so to speak, "as we be" and so will never be Galahad.

The ambiguities of Lancelot's character are expressed very clearly by a hermit in conversation with Gawain:

For I dare sey, as synfull as ever sir Launcelot hath byn, sith that he wente into the queste of the Sankgreal he slew never man nother nought shall, tylle that he com to Camelot agayne; for he hath takyn upon hym to forsake synne. And nere were that he ys nat stable, but by hys thoughte he ys lyckly to turne agayne, he sholde be nexte to encheve hit sauff sir Galahad, hys sonne; but God knowith hys thought and hys unstablenesse. And yett shall he dye ryght an holy man, and no doute he hath no felow of none erthely synfull man lyvyng. (M. p. 948, ll. 20–29)

This passage is Malory's addition and presents both sides of Lancelot's character as Malory conceives him. He is praised for refraining from murder and thus living up to the standards of secular morality and brotherhood, and for taking upon himself a life of repentance, forsaking sin. This sets him off from Gawain. Yet Lancelot is unstable; this appears to be for Malory his main fault, a fault not mentioned in the *Queste*. He cannot hold steadfastly to the spiritual path like Galahad but "ys lyckly to turne agayne." Nonetheless, Malory cannot forbear referring to Lancelot's holy end, a statement also absent in the

Queste, in an effort to mitigate the knight's present wrongs, and Malory repeats that Lancelot is the best of any "erthely synfull man lyvyng." It is this admixture of qualities that makes Lancelot's struggle of concern to Malory; by it Lancelot is "like us." Lancelot's instability is, in fact, the only explanation for the remarkable addition Malory makes at the beginning of the last Lancelot section, while Lancelot is on the boat that carries the body of Perceval's sister. Although dwelling in spiritual bliss on the boat, "on a nyght he wente to play hym by the watirs syde, for he was somwhat wery of the shippe" (M. p. 1011, l. 31–p. 1012, l. 1). An impossible occurrence in the *Queste*, Lancelot's apparent boredom with passive attendance upon God's commands illustrates his spiritual instability.

The last Lancelot section, which relates his Grail adventures, broadly follows the pattern of the *Queste*, but Malory makes a number of changes that strengthen Lancelot's role. He omits the hermit who comments on the knight's spiritual progress (Q. p. 248, l. 3–p. 249, l. 23 [pp. 255–56]), probably because for Malory Lancelot's presence on the boat with the body of Perceval's sister is sufficient commentary on his improved state. When Galahad enters the boat and asks Lancelot's name, Malory has him add, "For much my herte gevith unto you" (M. p. 1012, ll. 11–12), an expression of filial sentiment not found in the French. In Malory when Galahad learns who Lancelot is, "he kneled downe and askyd hym hys blyssynge" (M. p. 1012, l. 18). These additions tend to enhance Lancelot's stature by identifying him as Galahad's progenitor and thus deserving of his son's respect and affection. In addition, Lancelot partakes thereby of Galahad's glory.

In fact, throughout Malory's work Galahad's role is diminished except in relation to Lancelot. For example, when Lancelot and Galahad must part, in the *Queste* Lancelot asks Galahad to pray for him, and Galahad replies that only Lancelot's own prayers will avail him (Q. p. 252, ll. 26–27 [p. 259]). In Malory the direction is entirely changed; Lancelot says, "Now, my sonne, sir Galahad, sith we shall departe and nother of us se other more, I pray to that Hyghe Fadir, conserve me and you bothe." Although Galahad still replies that "no prayer avaylith so much as youres" (M. p. 1013, l. 31–p. 1014, l. 2), there is a subtle but important difference. Lancelot gains in dignity by praying for both of them rather than beseeching Galahad to pray for him, and instead of reprimanding Lancelot, Galahad acknowledges the efficacy of Lancelot's prayer.

Malory closely translates Lancelot's experiences in the Grail Castle at Corbenic. Lancelot enters the castle, sees the priest holding up the body of Christ, rushes forward to help him, and falls into a trance for twenty-four days. Upon awakening, when those gathered about ask what he has seen, Lancelot responds, "I have sene . . . grete mervayles that no tunge may telle, and more than ony herte can thynke. And had nat my synne bene beforetyme, ellis I had sene muche more" (M. p. 1017, ll. 11–13). These passages are close renderings of Malory's source. However, he has abbreviated both, leaving out material indicating that spiritual blindness prevented Lancelot from seeing more. In the *Queste* after the first passage, Lancelot says that his vision was incomplete because of "ma veue conchiee de la tres grant ordure dou monde fu essorbee" (Q. p. 258, ll. 3–4) [my eyes blinded, that had been sullied by looking on the midden of this world (p. 264)]. And from the second passage, Malory deletes "se ne fust que je perdi la veue de mes euz et le pooir dou cors, por la grant desloiauté que Diex avoit veue en moi" (Q. p. 258, ll. 11–13) [had I not lost the sight of my eyes and all power over my body, on account of the infamy that God had seen in me (p. 264)]. For Malory it is not Lancelot's blindness, a spiritual condition, that caused his vision to be partial but instead his past failure to exhibit right behavior.

Nonetheless, Malory implies in his work that Lancelot's vision of the Grail secrets is far more complete than it is in his source. In the *Queste* the people of the castle tell Lancelot that he may as well leave off the hair shirt, for his quest is over (Q. p. 259, ll. 1–4 [p. 265]). Their words, in fact, imply failure. They express a desire to see those who can truly achieve the Grail (Q. p. 259, ll. 4–5 [p. 265]). In Malory, however, it is Lancelot's success in seeing something of the Grail that dominates: "Sir

. . . the queste of the Sankgreall ys encheved now ryght in you, and never shall ye se of Sankgreall more than ye have sene" (M. p. 1017, l. 30–p. 1018, l. 2). Malory's rendering is thus more positive than his source; while the *Queste* stresses Lancelot's present failure and the futility of his ever coming closer to the Grail, Malory's version emphasizes the knight's success in achieving as much as he has and, indeed, gives the impression that it is not so bad never to "se of Sankgreall more than ye have sene." Lancelot's response shows him also to be quite satisfied with his accomplishment: "Now I thanke God . . . for Hys grete mercy of that I have sene, for hit suffisith me. For, as I suppose, no man in thys worlde have lyved bettir than I have done to enchyeve that I have done" (M. p. 1018, ll. 3–6). And he is right; he has lived better than any man in this world, according to Malory's standards of ideal chivalry. He is brave and noble, demonstrates knightly brotherhood and avoids murder, and for the most part lives a life consistent with the standards of normal Christian morality. He has sinned by undertaking wrong battles for the sake of love, but he has since confessed and done penance, and for this he is in Malory rewarded by ranking not quite with the elect knights but far closer to them than he does in the *Queste*. His vision of the Grail secrets is not complete—he is still unstable; Lancelot is not Galahad, nor even Bors or Perceval. Nonetheless, Malory has shown what can be accomplished by the best of those who are of this earth, if they take great pain upon themselves. Malory's Lancelot has a right to be content, and he demonstrates his own understanding of exactly what he has accomplished when he says, "for hit suffisith me"—"the queste of the Sankgreall ys encheved now ryght" in him.

At the end of this section in the *Queste*, Lancelot returns to Arthur's court and is received joyfully by all. Yet the section plays out on a dark note: few others have yet returned, and those who had come back had failed in the quest (Q. p. 262, ll. 17–18 [p. 268]). Malory expands this homecoming, increases Lancelot's role in it, and eliminates the sense of failure which overshadows Arthur's court in the *Queste*:

And there had he grete chere all that nyght, and on the morne he turned to Camelot where he founde kynge Arthure and the quene.

But many of the knyghtes of Rounde Table were slayne and destroyed, more than halff; and so three of them were com home, sir Ector, Gawayne, and Lyonell, and many other that nedith nat now to reherce. And all the courte were passyng glad of sir Launcelot, and the kynge asked hym many tydyngis of hys sonne sir Galahad.

And there sir Launcelot tolde the kynge of hys aventures that befelle hym syne he departed. And also he tolde hym of the aventures of sir Galahad, sir Percivale, and sir Bors whych that he knew by the lettir of the ded mayden, and also as sir Galahad had tolde hym.

"Now God wolde," seyde the kynge, "that they were all three here!"

"That shall never be," seyde sir Launcelot, "for two of hem shall ye never se. But one of them shall com home agayne." (M. p. 1020, ll. 17–34)

Malory nowhere recalls the shame that shall forever accompany the knights of the *Queste* for their failure to achieve the Grail, nor does he even mention the failure itself. He is far more concerned with the temporal fates of the members of the Round Table ("But many of the knyghtes of Rounde Table were slayne and destroyed, more than halff") than with passing spiritual judgment on Arthur's court. This is not surprising, for Malory's emphasis on the earthly brotherhood of knights has been dominant throughout his work. He diverges from his source in locating the tragedy of the end of the quest; it is not that the majority of the knights of the Round Table fail to meet the spiritual standards set by the appearance of the Grail but that so many die in the attempt to achieve it. That Lancelot is very much a part of the knightly brotherhood and is in fact preeminent in it is evident when he relates the adventures of the others. He is even the spokesman for the elect who do not return: not only does he relate the adventures of Galahad, Perceval, and Bors; he also tells the court of their ultimate fates, thus becoming the bearer of privileged information, a task reserved to Bors in the *Queste*. Besides this further emphasis on Lancelot, Malory's elaboration on this scene also brings Arthur's court into a closer relationship to the quest itself than it has in the *Queste*. The scene is the culmination of Malory's development of the possibilities for excellence within the standards of Round Table chivalry. Lancelot, the best of any earthly sinful man, returns from the quest to relate all but the final Grail adventures and thus binds together the Arthurian and Grail worlds through his person and his report.

Following Galahad's final achievement of the Grail, in bidding farewell to Bors, Malory has Galahad send greetings to Lancelot as he does in the *Queste*. But Malory adds, "and as sone as ye se hym bydde hym remembir of this worlde unstable" (M. p. 1035, ll. 11–12). Lancelot's greatest flaw is instability, and because of it his vision of the Grail was incomplete. Yet when Bors returns to court and Arthur wishes to have the Grail adventures chronicled, Bors "tolde hym of the hyghe aventures of the Sankgreall such as had befalle hym and his three felowes, which were sir Launcelot, Percivale, and sir Galahad and hymselff" (M. p. 1036, ll. 17–19). Here Lancelot is included among the elect knights. It is clear that for Malory, the best knight—earthly and sinful though he may be—deserves inclusion in this company, for although he is not the best spiritually, he is the best example of chivalry Arthur's court can claim. More remarkable still than Lancelot's place among the elect knights is the statement that "than sir Launcelot tolde the adventures of the Sangreall that he had sene" (M. p. 1036, ll. 19–20). In the *Queste* Lancelot had a glimpse of that which he was unworthy to view *apertement*, whereas here the implication is that he has seen far more than in the *Queste*. Of course, in Malory as in the French, Lancelot was not present at Sarras for the final Grail adventures. Nonetheless, the statement indicates that for Malory Lancelot's experience is worthy of record; it does not in any way imply that either Lancelot or those present believe that he is relating a failure.

With the statement that these adventures were recorded and placed in the library at Salisbury, the *Queste* ends. However, at this point Malory invents a dialogue between Bors and Lancelot which presents Lancelot at his best and also mitigates the finality felt at the end of the *Queste* by demonstrating that brotherly affection shall endure even though the Grail has disappeared and the quest for it is over:

And anone sir Bors seyde to sir Launcelot,

"Sir Galahad, youre owne sonne, salewed you by me, and aftir you my lorde kynge Arthure and all the hole courte, and so ded sir Percivale. For I buryed them both myne owne hondis in the cité of Sarras. Also, sir Launcelot, sir Galahad prayde you to remembir of thys unsyker worlde, as ye behyght hym whan ye were togydirs more than halffe a yere."

"Thys ys trew," seyde sir Launcelot, "now I truste to God hys prayer shall avayle me."

Than sir Launcelot toke sir Bors in hys armys and seyde,

"Cousyn, ye ar ryght wellcom to me! For all that ever I may do for you and for yours, ye shall fynde my poure body redy atte all tymes whyle the spyryte is in hit, and that I promyse you feythfully, and never to fayle. And wete ye well, gentyl cousyn sir Bors, ye and I shall never departe in sundir whylis oure lyvys may laste."

"Sir," seyde he, "as ye woll, so woll I." (M. p. 1036, l. 23–p. 1037, l. 7)

The addition reaffirms the values of loyal brotherhood Malory has emphasized throughout the *Sankgreal* and reconfirms Lancelot as the prime exemplar of them among mortal knights. The Grail may be gone, but the brotherhood of chivalry remains. Galahad, the only true representative of transcendent spirituality, is also gone; yet men of good will, like Lancelot and Bors, remain to carry on the struggle on the side of the morally right. [14] Malory's ending reestablishes the society of the Round Table as a good to be preserved. Even Bors's report of Galahad's greetings to those of Arthur's court confers value on that fellowship, for in the *Queste* Galahad sends greetings only to Lancelot. It is true that in Malory Galahad bids Lancelot to "remembir of thys unsyker worlde," but Lancelot himself, before the quest began, attempted to diminish Arthur's grief at their departure by saying, "for of dethe we be syker" (M. p. 867, l. 12). But even with this "unsyker" world, where death is the only surety, one can attain to excellence by conduct that betokens moral and brotherly values. However, Malory's standards are designed for life here on earth and do not require denial of earthly life in favor of heavenly; obviously, he recognizes the transcendent spirituality personified in Galahad, but the emphases found throughout his work make it clear that this is not his main concern. Rather, in order that his adaptation of the Grail story should effectively express what is important to him, Malory extols Lancelot, "the best of ony synfull man of the worlde."

ing of the Grail by demonstrating its significance in sacred history; by means of *digressio* the present moment expands to include the past, while at the same time the past converges on the present, lending to events a significance far beyond their immediate import. Galahad's achievement of the Grail gains in meaning by being foreshadowed and prepared for by events in sacred history as momentous as Christ's coming and as far back as Adam and Eve. For Malory, however, the present moment is important in itself; therefore, he systematically either excises or radically reduces all the digressions in his source. Since his concern lies with the possibilities for worthiness by the best the world has to offer, as exemplified in the fellowship of the Round Table, such digressions for him divert attention from the circumscribed world in which his action takes place. The significance of Malory's story does not derive from historical reverberation but lies within men themselves.

Similarly, Malory follows Geoffrey's dictum to "Give no quarter to *repetition*." In the *Queste*, *interpretatio*, or repetition, is the means whereby events are repeated on various levels— adventure, dream, vision, and allegorical explication. The author of the *Queste* uses repetition to elaborate on the meaning of the Grail through narrative; each repetition of an event in a different mode reveals some aspect of the Grail's meaning in the response it elicits. Malory almost totally eliminates allegory, in conformity with his understanding of the quest as a literal event occurring in a particular time and place and involving earthly men. The quest becomes a chivalric adventure—special, to be sure, but distinguished from other adventures more in prominence than in kind. The allegorical explications in Malory's source remove the quest to a plane on which the values of secular chivalry no longer obtain; because Malory's interest lies in demonstrating the worthiness of these values, he limits the work to literal human action.

Malory's treatment of the Grail itself further demonstrates his concerns with men on earth. Just as he alters the dynamic amplifications of narrative in his source by eliminating historical digressions and allegories, he also alters the *Queste*'s static amplification of the Grail as description. His changes in the description of the Grail pare away the multiple attributes attached to it. Where in the French the Grail is presented as possessing diverse qualities and is described by means of various images, Malory retains attributes appropriate only to the Eucharistic vessel. The myriad images and qualities attached to the Grail in the *Queste* are an admirable means to demonstrate its ultimate ineffability as the symbol of the highest religious experience. The quest itself is undertaken to gain insight into this mystery, the substance of which can never be expressed but only gradually and partially adumbrated. Malory's Grail, however, is not this mystical symbol of the *Queste*; it is rather a religious object, a means of communion between God and man and available to all who prove themselves worthy according to ordinary standards of Christian morality. The Grail's quest is undertaken for reasons other than those in Malory's source. His Grail is presented from the beginning of this work as complete, with all the attributes it will ever have. It is the Eucharistic vessel; although it contains a most sacred Christian mystery, the quest is not undertaken to gain insight into that mystery. Instead, in Malory the quest serves as a vehicle to test the knightliness—in the sense of Christian chivalry constantly set forth by Malory—of the members of the Round Table. The adventures encountered by the knights are not shadows of transcendent reality but are real adventures that prove their mettle. Lancelot establishes his worth not by passively putting down his arms in a symbolic gesture of submission to God's will before the River Marcoise but by crossing the river and thanking God for the adventure. It is action that counts with Malory, not spiritual condition; or rather, action is an indicator of spiritual condition or worthiness to achieve the Grail.[2]

The revised standards permit Malory's Lancelot to come far closer to full achievement of the Grail than he does in the *Queste*. As we have seen by an analysis of Malory's use of emphasis, worthy knights are those who engage in morally right action and who uphold the values of brotherhood and fellowship; they use their prowess in support of these ideals and thus contribute to the strength and health of the Round

Table as a whole. Malory's admiration for the knights' brother-hood and for Lancelot in particular cause him to expand and enhance Lancelot's role, and to present him as the exemplar of these values. Lancelot is indeed flawed but far less so than in the *Queste*, and he emerges from his quest aware of what he has achieved and exhibiting the same nobility of spirit which characterizes him in all of Malory's tales. Malory's addition at the end of the *Sankgreal*, in which Lancelot expresses to Bors his undying friendship and loyalty, makes Lancelot the agent for what can almost be termed a happy ending.[3] Through him the Round Table has to a great degree proved its worth and viability, rather than as in the *Queste* having been held up to celestial standards and found sadly wanting. Malory's faith in the Round Table has—for the moment at least—been justi-fied.[4] If in the general joy and harmory at Arthur's court at the end of the *Sankgreal*, we detect discordant notes or intimations of tragedy, it is because we know how the whole story finally ends, as Malory surely also knew. Within this scene itself, however, there is nothing—except perhaps sorrow for the knights who have died in the quest—to indicate that the Round Table has entered its decline. Malory has thus adapted his source to give it a new meaning and significance; from a completely allegorical work whose adventures are a means to a partial discovery of a higher truth, he has fashioned a tale whose final goal becomes an excuse for the discovery, through adventure, of the good to which man can attain on earth.

This new meaning is achieved and revealed to us through structural transformation. Rhetorical abbreviation is the key to Malory's accomplishment. Whereas the *Queste* is composed according to principles of amplification, Geoffrey of Vinsauf's instructions on abbreviation aptly describe the process by which Malory altered his source. As we have seen, he does not simply shorten; specifically, Malory removes those elements that contribute to elaboration, and thus he does indeed "let the entire theme be confined within narrow limits." Those limits are the present time and place and the literal level. By judicious use of emphasis, he expands on the particulars he retains so that the focus of the work becomes the actions of men on earth.

This is in contrast to the *Queste*, in which literal action becomes a figure for doctrinal truth, and the present moment is fully integrated with all of sacred history, in effect dissolving into it. By narrowing the focus, Malory creates a work that is structurally the opposite of the *Queste*. His source is built within the *synecdochic* mode, wherein the whole is derived from the parts. Malory removes the "parts" by restriction of elaborating devices, by elimination of repetition, and by emphasis. In so doing, he arrives at a work that is direct rather than multileveled, and dramatic rather than intellectual and mystical. In short, he follows Geoffrey's instructions to "clear away mist and usher in sunlight."

Our insight into what Malory accomplished in his adaptation has been achieved by applying to the *Queste* and to Malory's *Sankgreal* the instructions on composition found in the medieval arts of poetry, the only compositional guides medieval writers were likely to know. Conclusions on Malory's art become more solid through an accurate understanding of the art of his sources. Thus the discussion of the *Queste* in chapter 3 attempts, by means of rhetorical analysis, to display the unique structural aspects of the *Queste*. The rhetorical principles used by its author are shown there analogous to the principles set forth by Paul Frankl to describe Gothic architecture: the rhetorical *synecdochic* mode corresponds to the architectural style of Partiality. However, the introduction of architectural principles into this study does not imply direct influence. It happens that the structural principles involved in those two kinds of artistic endeavor in the thirteenth century exhibit similar characteristics, and the architectural analogy helps to clarify the "shape" of a work of literature composed according to the principles of amplification. It has always been clear that the "shape" of Malory's *Sankgreal* differs from that of the *Queste*; for one obvious thing, it is shorter. It was this reduced size that suggested Malory's work could be explained in terms of rhetorical abbreviation. And the medieval arts of poetry provide a useful means of recognizing purpose in Malory's eliminations, changes, and additions. The validity of the conclusions drawn is thus supported by the fact that we are using identical terms of comparison; the arts of poetry provide a means to describe the compositional methods found in both the *Queste* and the *Sankgreal*.

This study does not claim to cover all aspects of Malory's art. For example, it does not touch on language or prose style. Neither is there any attempt to take note of or account for Malory's occasional nodding; it is true that he sometimes confuses names, sometimes muddles events, and even has a hermit interpret actions that he fails to include from his source. However, these lapses also reveal Malory's intent, for he never pays much attention to what he considers unimportant; thus if he is unclear as to whether Mordrain/Evelach is one or two persons, it does not really matter to him, since the incident is part of a digression, and Malory everywhere attempts to suppress digression.

This study has been focused on Malory's structural adaptation of the *Queste*. The underlying assumption is that an accurate understanding of structure reveals intent and meaning. The medieval arts of poetry provide means to understand the compositional principles by which many medieval writers worked, and hence to understand the structural variations found in their work. By the "symbolism of form," Paul Frankl means that the "shape" of a work can speak to us in and through itself. We have seen that in the *Queste* this is true: the *synecdochic* mode, corresponding to the architectural style of Partiality, is the structural equivalent for the partial illuminations of the meaning of the Grail which it is the author's intent to reveal. However, the "shape" of Malory's work speaks to us quite differently. By eliminating the proliferation of parts in the *Queste*, he realizes a work that is far more self-enclosed. This concentration of emphasis produces a work that corresponds remarkably closely to what Frankl describes as a style of Totality, a style that creates the opposite impression from that of Partiality. Architecture characterized by the style of Totality has frontal rather than diagonal views; one does not feel that the whole is constantly fading away into the unknown. Malory's elimination of repetition and digression has a similar effect in his work: events speak for themselves and are what they appear to be. Obviously, the analogy should not be carried too far; Malory's work and the architectural style of Totality—by which Frankl means Romanesque architecture—are not contemporaneous. Nonetheless, the general impressions received from the style of Totality—comprehensible, easily encompassed, and complete in itself—correspond both to Malory's structural narrowing and focusing as well as to his limiting thematic concerns to the struggles of Arthurian knights to be morally worthy. The symbolism of Malory's form speaks its own meaning through abbreviation: "The glory of a brief work consists in this: it says nothing more or less than is fitting" (*PN*, p. 42). If Malory has not created an elegant cathedral, with a complexity of perspectives that constantly reveal new insights as we move through it, he has very skillfully constructed "a castell in a valey, closed with a rennyng watir, whych had stronge wallis and hyghe" (M. p. 983, ll. 10–12). And it is, after all, castles in which knights live.

NOTES

BIBLIOGRAPHY

INDEX

Notes

CHAPTER I: PRINCIPLES OF ADAPTATION:
MEDIEVAL ARCHITECTURE AND POETICS

1   Eugène Vinaver, ed. *The Works of Sir Thomas Malory,* 3 vols., 2nd ed. (Oxford: Clarendon Press, 1967), p. 1534.
2   William Ryding, *Structure in Medieval Narrative* (The Hague: Mouton, 1971), p. 158.
3   Charles Moorman, in *The Book of Kyng Arthur: The Unity of Malory's* Morte Darthur (Lexington: University of Kentucky Press, 1965), compares Malory's entire work, including the *Sankgreal,* with its sources but makes no detailed study of the structure of these sources. His concern with the structure of Malory's work is limited to proving that it is tightly unified. More recently Mary Hynes-Berry briefly outlined some of the major structural differences between the *Sankgreal* and the *Queste* in "Malory's Translation of Meaning: *The Tale of the Sankgreal,*" *Studies in Philology,* 74 (1977), 243–57. See also Charles W. Whitworth, "The Sacred and the Secular in Malory's *Tale of the Sankgreal,*" *YES,* 5 (1975), 19–29.
4   Stephen Knight, *The Structure of Sir Thomas Malory's Arthuriad,* Australian Humanities Research Council Monograph 14 (Sydney: Sydney University Press, 1969), p. 60.

5 Ibid., p. 62.

6 For the proponents of unity in Malory, the guiding principle in his writing is the attempt to produce a coherent story from his diverse sources. The arguments of the strongest supporters of unity in Malory's work may be found in R. M. Lumiansky, ed. *Malory's Originality: A Critical Study of* Le Morte Darthur (Baltimore: The Johns Hopkins Press, 1964). For a list of other articles relating to the question of unity in Malory published by the contributors to *Malory's Originality*, see Knight, *Structure*, p. 15, n. 37. Recent scholarship tends to ignore the unity debate and refuses either to argue for unity or to maintain with Vinaver that Malory wrote eight books rather than one. This is a fruitful attitude, in that it frees scholars to examine other aspects of Malory's art. See especially Mark Lambert, *Malory: Style and Vision in* Le Morte Darthur (New Haven: Yale University Press, 1975), and Larry Benson, *Malory's* Morte Darthur (Cambridge, Mass.: Harvard University Press, 1976). Although unity is not an issue in my study, it is obvious that I believe one can legitimately study a single tale in itself without regard for the others, since I am confining my discussion to the relationship of Malory's *Sankgreal* to his French source, the *Queste del Saint Graal*.

7 Jean Frappier, *Etude sur La Mort Le Roi Artu*, 2nd ed. rev. and augmented (Geneva: Droz, 1968), pp. 142–46.

8 See Edgar de Bruyne's fundamental study of aesthetic correspondence in the Middle Ages, *Etudes d'esthétique médiévale*, 3 vols. (Bruges: De Tempel, 1946), and Eugène Vinaver, *The Rise of Romance* (Oxford: Clarendon Press, 1971), pp. 68–98. Hugh of St. Victor uses the architectural image to describe the allegorical structure of Scripture in *The Didascalicon*, trans. Jerome Taylor (New York: Columbia University Press, 1961), pp. 140–44. See in general Henri de Lubac, *Exégèse médiévale: les quartre sens de l'écriture* (Paris: Aubier, 1959–64), II, ii, 41–60, and Douglas Kelly, "Theory of Composition in Medieval Narrative Poetry and Geoffrey of Vinsauf's *Poetria Nova*," *Mediaeval Studies*, 31 (1969), 119–30. Useful work in this area has also been done by D. W. Robertson, Jr., *A Preface to Chaucer: Studies in Medieval Perspectives* (Princeton, N.J.: Princeton University Press, 1962), pp. 3–285; Robert Jordan, *Chaucer and the Shape of Creation* (Cambridge, Mass.: Harvard University Press, 1967), pp. 1–60; Charles Muscatine, *Chaucer and the French Tradition* (Berkeley and Los

Angeles: University of California Press, 1966), esp. pp. 166–73; and Norris J. Lacy, "Spatial Form in the *Mort Artu*," *Symposium*, 31, no. 4 (1977).

9   Geoffrey of Vinsauf, *Poetria Nova*, trans. Margaret F. Nims (Toronto: Pontifical Institute of Mediaeval Studies, 1967), pp. 16–17. Hereafter referred to in text as *PN*.

10 For a cogent discussion of the need to understand medieval literary structure in contemporary terms, see S. T. Knight, "Some Aspects of Structure in Medieval Literature," *Parergon*, 16 (1976), 3–17.

11 "Si quis habet fundare domum, non currit ad actum / Impetuosa manus: intrinseca linea cordis / Praemetitur opus, seriemque sub ordine certo / Interior praescribit homo, totamque figurat / Ante manus cordis quam corporis; et status ejus / Est prius archetypus quam sensilis. Ipsa poesis / Spectet in hoc speculo quae lex sit danda poetis. / Non manus ad calamum praeceps, non lingua sit ardens / Ad verbum: neutram manibus committe regendam / Fortunae; / sed mens discreta praeambula facti, / Ut melius fortunet opus, suspendat earum / Officium, tractetque diu de themate secum. / Circinus interior mentis praecircinet omne / Materiae spatium. Certus praelimitet ordo / Unde praearripiat cursum stylus, at ubi Gades / Figat. Opus totum prudens in pectoris arcem / Contrahe, sitque prius in pectore quam sit in ore." Geoffrey of Vinsauf, *Poetria Nova*, v. 43–59, in E. Faral, *Les arts poétiques du XIIe et du XIIIe siècle* (Paris: Champion, 1924), pp. 197–262.

12 Otto von Simson, *The Gothic Cathedral: Origins of Gothic Architecture and the Medieval Concept of Order*, 2nd ed. (New York: Harper and Row, 1962), p. 231. For thorough discussion of Chartrian poetics, and additional bibliography, see Winthrop Wetherbee, *Platonism and Poetry in the Twelfth Century* (Princeton, N.J.: Princeton University Press, 1972).

13 Erwin Panofsky, ed., *Abbot Suger on the Abbey Church of St.-Denis and its Art Treasures* (Princeton, N.J.: Princeton University Press, 1946).

14 For example, Wilhelm Worringer, in *Form in Gothic*, trans. Sir Herbert Read, rev. ed. (New York: Schocken Books, 1957), sees Gothic architecture as the projection of the spirit of Nordic Man, a mythic being who has no clear historical or geographical boundaries; whereas Arnold Hauser, in *The Social History of Art*, trans.

Stanley Godman (New York: Vintage Books, 1959), I, sees Gothic architecture as the result of socioeconomic forces where the cathedral-building is a collective effort, the authority having passed out of the hands of the clergy into those of the laity. Neither of these theories produces a useful description of the structural principles on which Gothic architecture is based, since in each the emphasis is on external factors. Numerous other theories designed to account for Gothic architecture since its beginning are presented by Paul Frankl in *The Gothic: Literary Sources and Interpretations through Eight Centuries* (Princeton, N.J.: Princeton University Press, 1960):

> For Romanticists Gothic was Catholic; for nationalists it was French (Celtic), English or German; for Socialists it is "collective." In any case the *value* of Gothic as a style which prevailed for four hundred years of the Middle Ages cannot be judged in any such way as this (p. 689).

15 Paul Frankl, *Gothic Architecture*, in *The Pelican History of Art*, ed. Nikolaus Pevsner, trans. Dieter Pevsner (Baltimore: Penguin Books, 1962).

16 Ibid., p. 13.

17 Ibid., p. 12.

18 Ibid.

19 Frankl, *The Gothic*, p. 822.

20 Ibid., p. 823.

21 Frankl, *Gothic Architecture*, p. 11.

22 While urging caution in *any* method of comparison among the arts, Wellek and Warren do concede that "the most central approach to a comparison of the arts is based on an analysis of the actual objects of art, and thus of their structural relationships." René Wellek and Austin Warren, *Theory of Literature*, 3rd ed., rev. (New York: A Harvest Book, 1956), p. 130.

23 See my "The Style of Partiality: Gothic Architecture and The Vulgate Cycle of Arthurian Romances," *Genre*, 6, No. 4 (1973), 376–87.

24 On this subject, see Douglas Kelly, "Topical Invention in Medieval French Literature," in *Medieval Eloquence: Studies in the Theory and Practice of Medieval Rhetoric*, ed. James J. Murphy (Berkeley and Los Angeles: University of California Press, 1978), pp. 231–51, and "*Matière* and *genera dicendi* in Medieval Romance," *Yale French Studies*, 51 (1974), 147–59. See also Vinaver, *The Rise of Romance*, ch. 4 and 5; *Works of Malory* lxxv ff; and Ernest Gallo,

"Matthew of Vendôme: Introductory Treatise on the Art of Poetry," *Proceedings of the American Philosophical Society*, 118 (1974), 54–55.

25 These principles apply to either verse or prose, and the distinction between them is irrelevant in this context. Ernst Robert Curtius, *European Literature and the Latin Middle Ages*, trans. Willard R. Trask (New York and Evanston: Harper and Row, 1953) p. 147: "Antiquity did not conceive of poetry and prose as two forms of expression differing in essence and origin. On the contrary, both fall within the inconclusive concept 'discourse'." Furthermore, Geoffrey of Vinsauf states that "the method of prose and verse does not differ; rather, the principles of art remain the same, whether in a composition bound by the laws of meter or in one independent of those laws, although what depends upon the principles of art is not always the same" (*PN*, p. 83). ("Cetera non variat ratio, sed, carmine metri / Legibus astricto vel ab ejus lege soluto, / Ars eadem semper, quamvis quod pendet ab arte / Non sit semper idem" [*Poetria Nova*, v. 1878–81]). After enunciating some of the ornaments of style, Geoffrey sums up: "Now I have provided a comb: if they are groomed with it, compositions, whether in prose or verse, will gleam with elegance" (*PN*, p. 86). ("Ecce dedi pecten, quo si sint pexa relucent / Carmina tam prosae quam metra" [*Poetria Nova*, v. 1948–49]).

26 That the Vulgate *Queste del Saint Graal* is the sole source for Malory's *Tale of the Sankgreal* has been firmly established by Vinaver; see *Works of Malory*, pp. 1534–35.

27 Gallo, "Matthew of Vendôme," p. 52.

28 Ibid.

29 Ibid., p. 53.

30 Ernest Gallo, "The *Poetria Nova* of Geoffrey of Vinsauf," in *Medieval Eloquence*, ed. Murphy, p. 52.

31 "Geoffrey's conception of composition was widespread among twelfth and thirteenth century writers, and his conception demanded that disposition and ornamentation be subordinate to and to a large extent determined by the requirements of the subject matter and design of the poem," Kelly, "Theory of Composition," pp. 140–41.

32 Gallo, "Matthew of Vendôme," p. 54.

33 Jane Baltzell Kopp stresses the importance of amplification and abbreviation to the entire structure of a work in "Rhetorical 'Am-

plification' and 'Abbreviation' and the Structure of Medieval Narrative," *Pacific Coast Philology*, 2 (April, 1967), 32–39.

34   Gallo, "Matthew of Vendôme," p. 51; for the distinctions between medieval grammar and rhetoric, see Douglas Kelly, "The Scope and Treatment of Composition in the Twelfth and Thirteenth-Century Arts of Poetry," *Speculum*, 41 (1966), 261–78.

35   Gallo, "Matthew of Vendôme," p. 51; Kelly, "Scope and Treatment," p. 262.

36   Ibid., pp. 58–59.

37   Douglas Kelly, "The Source and Meaning of *conjointure* in Chrétien's *Erec* 14," *Viator*, 1 (1970), 183.

38   Kelly, "Theory of Composition," p. 124, n. 16.

39   Geoffrey of Vinsauf, *Documentum de modo et arte dictandi et versificandi*, trans. with an intro. by Roger P. Parr (Milwaukee: Marquette University Press, 1968), II. 3. C. 134.

40   Vinaver, *The Rise of Romance*, p. 20.

41   Ibid., p. 22.

42   Gallo, "Matthew of Vendôme," p. 53.

43   *Documentum*, II. 3. C. 133: "Primus modus est ne moremur ubi moram faciunt alii; sed, ubi moram faciunt, transeamus, ubi transeunt, moram faciamus."

44   Vinaver, *The Rise of Romance*, p. 81.

45   "Geoffrey (in the *Poetria Nova, ca.* 1210, and the *Documentum*); Eberhard the German (in the *Laborintus*, 1210–1280); and John of Garland (in the *Poetria*, after 1229) give the following methods of achieving Amplification: Synonymy, Circumlocution, Apostrophe, Prosopopeia, Description, and Digression. The *Poetria Nova* and the *Laborintus* add Comparison and Contraries (*oppositio*)." Ernest Gallo, *The* Poetria Nova *and its Sources in Early Rhetorical Doctrine* (The Hague: Mouton, 1971), p. 155.

46   "Multiplice forma / Dissimuletur idem; varius sit et tamen idem" (*Poetria Nova*, v. 224–25).

47   Alain de Lille, *The Complaint of Nature*, trans. Douglas M. Moffat (New York: Henry Holt, 1908), p. 25.

48   "Nec plane detege, sed rem / Innue per notulas; nec sermo perambulet in re, / Sed rem circuiens longis ambagibus ambi / Quod breviter dicturus eras" (*Poetria Nova*, v. 230–33).

49   *La Queste del Saint Graal*, ed. Albert Pauphilet (Paris: Champion, 1949), p. 161, l. 33—p. 162, l. 2; *The Quest of the Holy Grail*, trans. with an intro. by P. M. Matarasso (Baltimore: Penguin Books, 1969), p. 175. Subsequent references are to these texts.

50 "Materiae fines exi paulumque recede / Et diverte stylum; sed nec divertere longe / Unde gravet revocare gradum. . . . Est etiam quaedam digressio quando propinqua / Transeo, quod procul est praemittens ordine verso" (*Poetria Nova*, v. 533–35, 537–38).

51 "modis dictis a partibus innuo totum" (*Poetria Nova*, v. 1034).

52 "Si brevis esse velis, prius ista priora recide, / Quae pompam faciunt; modicumque prematur in orbem / Summula materiae, quam tali comprime lege: / Plurima perstringat paucis expressa locutrix / Emphasis; . . . —Respuat audiri bis idem;—prudentia docti / In dictis non dicta notet; . . . —Vel manus artificis multas ita conflet in unam, / Mentis ut intuitu multae videantur in una" (*Poetria Nova*, v. 695–699, 702–3, 705–6).

53 "Non superinfundat nubem, sed nube remota / Inducat solem" (*Poetria Nova*, v. 710–11).

54 Paul Frankl, *Principles of Architectural History: The Four Phases of Architectural Style, 1420–1900*, trans. and ed. by James F. O'Gorman (Cambridge, Mass.: The MIT Press, 1968).

55 Frankl, *Gothic Architecture*, pp. 212–14.

56 Edward D. Kennedy, "Malory and his English Sources," in *Aspects of Malory*, ed. Toshiyuki Takamiya and Derek Brewer (Cambridge: D. S. Brewer; Woodbridge, Suffolk: Boydell & Brewer; Totowa, N.J.: Rowman & Littlefield, 1981), p. 28.

57 The terms "static" and "dynamic" are borrowed from Marc-René Jung, *Etudes sur le poème allégorique en France au moyen age*, Romanica Helvetica, 82 (Bern: Francke, 1971), p. 20.

CHAPTER II:
THE GRAIL IN THE QUESTE AND MALORY

1 "Sic surgit permulta seges de semine pauco: / Flumina magna trahunt ortus de fonte pusillo, / De tenui virga grandis protenditur arbor" (*Poetria Nova*, v. 692–94).

2 For a review of the literature on these and other more arcane definitions of the Grail, see Frederick William Locke, "A New Approach to the Study of the *Queste del Saint Graal*," *Romanic Review*, 45 (1954), 241–50. Locke states, quite correctly, that "the Grail is not one thing to the exclusion of any other. That is to say, it cannot be *equated* with something else" (p. 244). Rosemond Tuve similarly says, "I suppose it is not necessary to underline

the fact that the images [in medieval allegory] do not *equate with* the concepts spoken of (if this were so, no images would be needed)," in *Allegorical Imagery: Some Mediaeval Books and Their Posterity* (Princeton, N.J.: Princeton University Press, 1966), p. 21.

3 See Kelly, *"Matière,"* p. 158.

4 Charles Moorman has noted in *The Book of Kyng Arthur* that "Malory wishes to make the Grail itself tangible and concrete without diminishing in the least its mystical qualities" (p. 36).

5 Malory's emphasis on brotherhood is examined in chapter 4.

6 In both Malory and the *Queste*, of course, Gawain because of his unworthiness never sees anything of the Grail, nor does he participate in adventures connected with it. See also Pauline Matarasso, *The Redemption of Chivalry: A Study of the* Queste Del Saint Graal (Geneva: Droz, 1979), pp. 180–204.

7 *Works of Malory*, p. xci.

8 In this scene in Malory, as in the *Queste*, the Grail moves of its own accord, but because of the general reduction of mysterious elements in Malory, and his matter-of-fact reporting of events, the ability of the Grail to appear and disappear is taken quite for granted; it is simply something that God can do.

9 Malory does retain *circumlocutio* as a narrative technique in the ordering of the knights' adventures; yet whereas the *Queste* also uses this device to describe the Grail itself, Malory does not.

CHAPTER III: DYNAMIC AMPLIFICATION:
NARRATIVE AND MEANING
IN LA QUESTE DEL SAINT GRAAL

1 See Jean Frappier, "Le Graal et la chevalerie," *Romania*, 75 (1954), 165–210.

2 Aside from Frederick William Locke's discussion of the scriptural and ritual patterns unifying the work in *The Quest for the Holy Grail: A Literary Study of a Thirteenth-Century French Romance* (Stanford, Calif.: Stanford University Press, 1960), there have been few strictly structural studies of the *Queste*. Matarasso's *Redemption of Chivalry* reveals how profoundly the *Queste*'s structure reflects scriptural truths and "that the author's belief in the historical reality of the Incarnation and Redemption allows him to embody their meaning in his work and thus extend the echoes of fiction to the farthest limits of Christian experience" (p. 243). Her

thorough and convincing study of the *Queste*'s allegory does not, however, deal with the literary means by which the author accomplishes these ends. Grace Armstrong Savage's 1973 Princeton University Ph.D. dissertation, "Narrative Techniques in the *Queste del Saint Graal*," does view the *Queste* as a "literary construct" and examines it from the perspective of the romance tradition. Yet *Queste* scholarship has largely concentrated on other areas of concern. For example, a good deal of attention has been given to defining the theology and doctrine of the *Queste*, and thus to the discovery of what the Grail itself means; see Locke, *Holy Grail*, pp. 241–50, especially p. 245, notes 7–13. Although Albert Pauphilet's *Etudes sur la Queste del Saint Graal attribuée à Gautier Map* (Paris: Champion, 1968) established the Cistercian influence on the work, the uniqueness of the *Queste* as both a romance and a theological exposition has also been examined in a few studies. Alexandre Micha, in "Etudes sur le Lancelot en prose: l'esprit du Lancelot-Graal," *Romania*, 82 (1961), 357–78, and Jean Frappier in "Le Graal" have demonstrated how the author of the *Queste* successfully united the previously separate stories of the Grail and Lancelot; while Helen Hennessy, in "The Uniting of Romance and Allegory in *La Queste del Saint Graal*," *Boston University Studies in English*, 4, (1960), 189–201, has examined the fusion of courtly and contemplative sources of medieval inspiration in the *Queste*. Despite the lack of a structural examination of the *Queste* itself, a good deal of work has been devoted to the structure of the Vulgate Cycle as a whole, including the *Queste*, especially since 1918 when Ferdinand Lot discovered the principle of *entrelacement* (*Etude sur le Lancelot en prose*, Paris: Champion, 1918), the interweaving of various narrative threads, each of which may be picked up and dropped in turn. The implications of this discovery have been most fully elaborated by Eugène Vinaver. See his *The Rise of Romance*, pp. 68–98; *Form and meaning in Medieval Romance* (Cambridge: Modern Humanities Research Association, 1966); and *A la recherche d'une poétique médiévale* (Paris: Nizet, 1970), pp. 129–49. Analysis of this compositional principle has been continued by Fanni Bogdanow in her work on the Post-Vulgate Cycle of Arthurian romance, *The Romance of the Grail: A Study of the Structure and Genesis of a Thirteenth-Century Arthurian Prose Romance* (Manchester: Manchester University Press; New York: Barnes and Noble, 1966). Rosemond Tuve's discussion of the *Queste*'s allegory, *Allegorical*

11 Tzvetan Todorov, *Poétique de la prose* (Paris: Editions du Seuil, 1971), p. 147.

12 Paul Zumthor, *Essai de poétique médiévale* (Paris: Editions du Seuil, 1972), p. 356.

13 See Tuve, *Allegorical Imagery*, p. 345: "one 'achieved' the Grail not by fighting for possession of it or protection of it but by trying to understand what it meant."

14 Todorov, *Poétique*, p. 143.

15 See also Erich Köhler on the typical return to the court: "Le retour de chevalier à la cour lorsqu'il est sorti victorieux de l'aventure, c'est-à-dire lorsque sa *queste* est achevée, la *Joie* de la cour devant ce retour, apportent la confirmation de l'acte qu'il a accompli pour lui-même et pour la communauté": *L'aventure chevaleresque: Idéal et reálité dans le roman courtois*, trans. Eliane Kaufholz (Paris: Gallimard, 1974), p. 96.

16 In her discussion of Arthurian tragedy in Malory, Maureen Fries also notes that Galahad's success does not lead to "communal salvation" but to "individual beatitude" ("Tragic Pattern in Malory's *Morte Darthur*: Medieval Narrative as Literary Myth," *The Early Renaissance* [Acta 5], ed. Aldo S. Bernardo [Binghamton Center for Medieval and Early Renaissance Studies: State University of New York: 1979], p. 91).

17 Erich Auerbach, *Mimesis: The Representation of Reality in Western Literature*, trans. Willard Trask (Garden City, N.Y.: Doubleday, 1957), p. 119.

18 Vinaver, *Form and Meaning*, p. 8.

19 Köhler, *L'aventure*, chaps. 3 and 6.

20 Ibid.: "La grâce n'est plus la récompense d'une aventure brillamment réussie, mais la condition nécessaire à l'aventure suprême susceptible de résoudre la tension entre l'homme et Dieu devenue insupportable: l'aventure du Graal," p. 224.

21 Todorov, *Poétique*, p. 139.

22 This is true even at the Grail castle, where Lancelot draws his sword to defend himself from the lions guarding the gate (p. 253, ll. 16–19 [p. 260]) and where he attempts to help the priest for whom Christ's body appears too heavy (p. 255, ll. 26–30 [p. 262]). In both instances God punishes him.

23 Pauphilet, *Etudes*, p. 131.

24 Ibid.

25 Ibid.

26 Ibid., p. 132.
27 Ibid., p. 133.
28 Ibid., p. 129.
29 Ibid.
30 Cf. the exception of the black and white birds in the Bors section (p. 170, l. 30–p. 171, l. 13 [pp. 183–84]), which demonstrates Bors's superior perception.
31 Cf. Gawain's earlier question to a hermit, "par ceste reson que vos me dites m'est il avis que puis que no serions en pechié mortel, por noiant irions avant en ceste Queste; car je n'i feroie noiant," (p. 161, ll. 7–10) [by reason of what you say it seems to me that since we should be in mortal sin, it would be pointless for us to pursue this Quest any further; for I should accomplish nothing (p. 174)], and the hermit's reply, "Certes . . . vos dites voir" (p. 161, l. 10) [Indeed, you speak the truth (p. 174)].
32 Charlotte C. Morse, *The Pattern of Judgment in the* Queste *and* Cleanness (Columbia: University of Missouri Press, 1978): "in the Grail quest Lancelot sees and knows as much as he is capable of seeing and knowing, and his capacity is not negligible" (p. 59).
33 *L'anemi* is a key word in the *Queste*; in contrast to Hector's failure, Bors and Perceval both triumphed over *l'anemi*'s attempted seductions.
34 Vinaver, *Rise of Romance*, p. 92. The principle is similar to that found by Henri Focillon in medieval ornament, which he says, "has given birth to an entire flora and fauna of hybrids that are subject to the laws of a world distinctly not our own." And he goes on to say that "Engendered by the motions of an imaginary space, these figures would be so absurd in the ordinary regions of life that they would not be permitted to exist. . . ." *The Life of Forms in Art*, trans. Charles Beecher Hogan and George Kubler (New York: Wittenborn, Shultz, 1948), p. 19.
35 Cf. Köhler, *L'aventure*: "Les chevaliers de la Table ronde sont tous de même rang, mais non pas de même nature," p. 104.
36 Gallo, "Matthew of Vendôme," p. 71.
37 The eight sections are in order: I. p. 32, l. 6–p. 35, l. 12 [pp. 58–60]; II. p. 74, l. 20–p. 79, l. 3 [pp. 97–101]; III. p. 83, l. 21–p. 86, l. 32 [pp. 105–8]; IV. p. 134, l. 13–p. 138, l. 8 [pp. 151–54]; V. p. 204, l. 5–p. 205, l. 4 [pp. 215–16]; VI. p. 206, l. 32–p. 209, l. 5 [pp. 218–20]; VII. p. 209, l. 9–p. 210, l. 4 [pp. 220–21]; and VIII. p. 210, l. 29–p. 226, l. 7 [pp. 222–35].
38 It may be noted here that the historical digressions are revealed

only to those who are worthy—Gawain and Hector have none—and only when they are ready to understand them; Perceval's simple faith and eager questions qualify him.

39 Hugh of St. Victor, describing the order of narration in the Bible, parallels closely Geoffrey's definition of *digressio* when he says that "the text of the Divine Page keeps neither to a natural nor to a continuous order of speech, both because it often places later things before early ones . . . and because it often connects even things which are separated from each other by an interval of time, as if one followed right on the heels of the other, so that it seems as if no lapse of time stood between those events which are set apart by no pause in the discourse" (*Didascalicon*, pp. 146–47).

40 See Vinaver, *Form and Meaning*.

41 Ibid., p. 24. See also Susanna Greer Fein, "Thomas Malory and the Pictorial Interlace of *La Queste del Saint Graal*," *University of Toronto Quarterly*, 46, No. 3 (Spring, 1977), 215–40, who states that "the wandering paths of the Arthurian knights seeking the Holy Grail can be regarded as a visual representation, a *pictorial interlace*, of the wandering through life of all mankind in search of divine salvation," p. 223.

42 For a discussion of artificial order as used and understood by medieval authors, see Gallo, "The *Poetria Nova*," in *Medieval Eloquence*, ed. Murphy, pp. 73–80; Kelly, "Topical Invention in Medieval French Literature" in ibid., pp. 242–45. For a history of the distinction in the Middle Ages, see Franz Quadlbauer, "Lukan im Schema des *ordo naturalis/artificialis*: ein Beiträg zur Geschichte der Lukanbewertung im lateinischen Mittelalter," *Grazer Beitrage*, 6 (1977), pp. 67–105.

43 John Leyerle, "The Interlace Structure of *Beowulf*," *University of Toronto Quarterly*, 37, No. 1 (1967), 8.

44 Vinaver, *Form and Meaning*, p. 24.

45 Tuve, *Allegorical Imagery*, p. 370.

46 Ibid, p. 364.

47 Ibid., p. 363.

48 Leyerle, "Interlace Structure," p. 8.

49 Focillon, *Life of Forms*, p. 3.

50 Chenu's discussion of the "symbolist mentality" of the latter half of the twelfth century reveals parallels with the mystery and ineffability of the Grail: "Connatural with matter, a man's intelligence had to work through matter to attain a grasp of transcendent realities, unknowable in themselves. . . . The symbol was

the means by which one could approach mystery; it was homo-
geneous with mystery and not a simple epistomological sign
more or less conventional in character." M.-D. Chenu, *Nature,
Man and Society in the Twelfth Century*, selected and trans. by
Jerome Taylor and Lester K. Little (Chicago: University of Chicago Press, 1968), p. 123.

51 See the Prologue to the *Estoire* added later to the Lancelot-Grail
cycle, in Sommer, ed., *Vulgate Version*, I, 5, ll. 1–16.

Chapter IV: Abbreviation and Meaning
in Malory's Tale of the Sankgreal

1 Vinaver states that Malory's "attitude may be described without
much risk of over-simplification as that of a man to whom the
quest of the Grail was primarily an *Arthurian* adventure and who
regarded the intrusion of the Grail upon Arthur's kingdom not as
a means of contrasting earthly and divine chivalry and condemning the former, but as an opportunity offered to the knights of the
Round Table to achieve still greater glory in *this* world," a view
that my examination of the work generally bears out. However,
Vinaver continues, "And so throughout the story Malory is primarily concerned with 'erthly worship,' not with any higher
purpose, and his one desire seems to be to secularize the Grail
theme as much as the story will allow" (*Works of Malory*, p. 1535).
This seems to me to go too far. Malory does not secularize the
story; rather, he exchanges mysticism and doctrine for Christian
moral behavior. In Malory men are not judged by what they
understand but by what they do. As Benson states, "Malory, like
Milton, was less concerned with the problems of a fugitive and
cloistered virtue than with the moral difficulties of this world, in
which both the spirit and the flesh have their necessary roles"
(*Malory's Morte Darthur*, p. 222).

2 In arguing for Malory's emphasis on Lancelot's and Galahad's
Arimathean ancestry, Valerie Lagorio states of this passage: "The
crux of the French version is to contrast Lancelot's human failings
with the perfection of his ancestral line, but Malory shifts the
emphasis to exalt his hero's inherited virtues and nobility." ("The
Glastonbury Legends and the English Arthurian Grail Romances," *Neuphilologische Mitteilungen*, 79 [1978], 364).

3 Cf. Q. p. 59, ll. 22–27 [p. 83]; M. p. 894–95.

4   Moorman is thus imprecise in stating that Malory "always pre-
serves the core of the French book's doctrinal statements, no
matter how great his deletions" (*The Book of Kyng Arthur*, p. 33).
What Malory does retain from the hermits' explications and sermons are those statements related to *moral* behavior, right and
wrong action.

5   This code of conduct is expressed in the oath King Arthur's
knights take every Pentecost: " . . . than the kynge stablysshed
all the knyghtes and gaff them rychesse and londys; and charged
them never to outerage nothir morthir, and allwayes to fle treson,
and to gyff mercy unto hym that askith mercy, uppon payne of
forfiture of their worship and lordship of kynge Arthure for
evirmore; and allwayes to do ladyes, damesels, and jantilwomen
and wydowes socour: strengthe hem in hir ryghtes, and never to
enforce them, uppon payne of dethe. Also that no man take no
batayles in a wrongefull quarell for no love ne for no worldis
goodis" (*Works of Malory*, p. 120, ll. 15–24).

 D. S. Brewer states, "For Malory—and we shall never understand him if we do not understand this—there is no essential
incompatibility between the values of Christianity and those of
the High Order of Knighthood, of ideal Arthurian chivalry" in
"the hoole book." In *Essays on Malory*, ed. J. A. W. Bennett
(Oxford: Clarendon Press, 1963), p. 58. Similarly, Vinaver says
that Malory "upholds knighthood, not as an ideal remote from
reality, nor as a moral doctrine in Caxton's sense, but as an issue
of immediate interest, related to memories of a recent past"
(*Works of Malory*, p. xxxiv). And Larry Benson finds in contemporary life a basis for Malory's merging of religious and chivalric
ideals: "By the fifteenth century, chivalry had become respectable
in the eyes of both Church and state, and the chivalric code of
Arthur's knights had become the ideal of an important segment
of society, that to which Malory and his noble readers belonged"
(*Malory's* Morte Darthur, p. 208).

6   This addition could indicate that Malory had access to a version of
the Post Vulgate *Queste*. Fanni Bogdanow describes the theme of
the Dolorous Stroke in the Post Vulgate Cycle thus: "It would
seem then, that the Dolorous Stroke theme occupies the key
position both in the *Suite du Merlin* and the Post Vulgate *Queste*.
The maiming of Pellean is the beginning of the adventures of
Logres; the healing of Pellean is the end. The episodes that
precede the maiming deal with the youth of Arthur and the early

years of his kingdom; those that follow the healing treat of its decay and end. The Lance begins to bleed only after the Dolorous Stroke; once the marvels are ended and Pellean healed it is appropriate that the Lance should disappear into Heaven. The healing of the Maimed King becomes Galaad's principal function; whereas in the Vulgate he is the New Lancelot, freed from the burden of sin that clogs his predecessor, and thus able to achieve the *visio Dei*, in the Post Vulgate *Queste* he is the counterpart of Balain, the Renewer who restores what the 'chevalier mescheans' had destroyed" (*The Romance of the Grail*, p. 137). Because Malory adds this description of the origin of the sword, his Galahad fulfills both of the roles Bogdanow outlines, and thus it is possible that his *Sankgreal* is influenced by the Post Vulgate *Queste*. However, since Malory had already drawn his Balin episode in the *Tale of King Arthur* from the *Suite du Merlin*, a work in which the Balin story serves largely as a prelude to the Post Vulgate *Queste*, he may have decided to include this description of the origin of the sword to give further significance to Galahad's quest—even though Balin never appears in the Vulgate Cycle, presumably Malory's only source for his *Sankgreal*. In any case, the function of this addition is not, as Moorman states, to serve as "the single most important linking of the Grail adventure with the whole of the *Morte Darthur*" (*The Book of Kyng Arthur*, p. 46); on the contrary, the addition of this description increases the self-sufficiency of the tale by providing explanation and thematic motivation within the confines of the tale itself.

See also Vinaver, "Landmarks in Arthurian Romance," in *The Expansion and Transformation of Courtly Literature*, ed. Nathaniel B. Smith and Joseph T. Snow (Athens: The University of Georgia Press, 1980), p. 28.

7 This statement is not in Malory's source, and places his Galahad even further beyond emulation than the French Galahad. In effect, he is almost dismissed in Malory.

8 Vinaver initially noted Malory's rehabilitation of Lancelot (*Works of Malory*, pp. 1536–37), and this view has largely been accepted. Benson states that "Malory removes much of the attack on Lancelot, thus considerably softening the effect of Lancelot's failure, and he adds many passages praising Lancelot, as if to assure his readers that Lancelot's failure in the spiritual quest does not diminish his knightly stature" (*Malory's* Morte Darthur, p. 218).

9 For a different view, see Moorman, who argues that Malory

"condemned the adultery which was an integral part of the system of courtly love as he found it reflected in his French sources." "*The Tale of the Sankgreall*: Human Frailty," in *Malory's Originality*, ed. R. M. Lamiansky (Baltimore: The Johns Hopkins Press, 1964), p. 192, n. 11.

10   Cf. P. J. C. Field: "His [Malory's] fundamental concern is to transmit his enthusiasm for knightliness"; and Field also states that "Life in the *Morte Darthur* is a moral matter, judged according to a chivalric code." *Romance and Chronicle: A Study of Malory's Prose Style* (Bloomington: Indiana University Press, 1971), p. 157.

11   That Malory has no interest in condemning Guinevere is also shown by his praise of true love at the beginning of the Knight of the Cart episode in Book VII, which he ends by saying of Guinevere, "that whyle she lyved she was a trew lover, and therefor she had a good ende" (*Works of Malory*, p. 1120, ll. 12–13).

12   Malory has the hermit give a brief interpretation of Galahad's part in Lancelot's dream, even though he eliminates Galahad's role in Lancelot's description of that dream. Although this may be partly due to oversight, it also indicates Malory's overriding concern for Lancelot.

13   This point is made in Douglas Kelly, "*Translatio Studii*: Translation, Adaptation, and Allegory in Medieval French Literature," *Philological Quarterly*, 57 (1978), 305.

14   Grace Armstrong Savage's examination of the relationship between Lancelot and Galahad concludes that Galahad is a natural choice to be the new anticourtly hero. However, she also states that "his respectful farewell to Lancelot suggests that the courtly hero and his world should not and cannot be forgotten" ("Father and Son in the *Queste del Saint Graal*," *Romance Philology*, 31 [1977], 16). Malory would agree, since he allows Galahad's farewell to authorize his own final scene.

CHAPTER V: THE SYMBOLISM OF FORM

1   See G. R. Simes, "Chivalry and Malory's Quest of the Holy Grail," *Parergon*, 17 (1977), 37–42.

2   See Benson: "Certainly Malory would not deny the values of the *Queste*, and to die 'ryght an holy man' was indeed devoutly to be wished. But Malory's ideal spiritual quest was much more that of the *Chemin de vaillance*, the 'worshipful way' that Lancelot follows

and thereby achieves the Heavenly City by way of earthly knight-hood" (*Malory's* Morte Darthur, p. 222). Similarly, D. S. Brewer: "Malory asserts the possibility that honour may be the same as goodness; that Christians may be good men, even if most of them do not want to be monks, and cannot be saints; and by a fruitful paradox of inconsistency he asserts the validity of this worldly ideal as well as of the transcendental ideal" (*Malory: The Morte Darthur*, ed. D. S. Brewer [Evanston, Ill.: Northwestern University Press, 1974], pp. 34–35).

3   "In his [Malory's] version there is no sense of finality, no implica-tion that an earlier way of life has been superseded. The Quest, in short, has not broken the Round Table. It was rather a special discipline for the knights from which they must necessarily re-turn to Camelot: the daily life of chivalry has still to be lived" (P. E. Tucker, "Chivalry in the *Morte*", in *Essays on Malory*, ed. Bennett.

4   Benson effectively demonstrates that comic elements inter-spersed with the historical tragic framework prevent Malory's work from becoming wholly tragic. Of the *Sankgreal* in particular, he states: "Yet, interwoven with the historical tragic narrative is a thematic 'comic' narrative, one of 'joy and great solace,' that leads to the vindication of Arthurian chivalry" (*Malory's* Morte Darthur, p. 209). See also Edward Kennedy, "English Sources," who suggests that Hardyng, the *Perlesvaus*, and the Prose *Tristan* provided Malory with examples "of a Grail story in which the Quest was compatible with Arthurian chivalry" (p. 46).

A Bibliography
of Works Cited

Primary Works

Alain de Lille. *The Complaint of Nature.* Trans. Douglas M. Moffat. New York: Holt, 1908.

Dante. *De vulgari eloquentia.* Ed. P. V. Mengaldo. Padua: Antenore, 1968.

Geoffrey of Vinsauf. *Documentum de modo et arte dictandi et versificandi.* In *Les arts poétiques du XIIe et du XIIIe siècle.* Ed. E. Faral. Paris: Champion, 1924, pp. 265–320.

Geoffrey of Vinsauf. *Documentum (Instruction in the Method and Art of Speaking and Versifying).* Trans. Roger P. Parr. Milwaukee: Marquette University Press, 1968.

Geoffrey of Vinsauf. *Poetria Nova.* In *Les arts poétiques du XIIe et du XIIIe siècle.* Ed. E. Faral. Paris: Champion, 1924, pp. 197–262.

Geoffrey of Vinsauf. *Poetria Nova.* Trans. Margaret F. Nims. Toronto: Pontifical Institute of Mediaeval Studies, 1967.

Hugh of St. Victor. *The Didascalicon.* Trans. Jerome Taylor. New York: Columbia University Press, 1961.

Malory, Sir Thomas. *The Works of Sir Thomas Malory.* Ed. Eugène Vinaver. 3 vols. 2nd ed. Oxford: Clarendon Press, 1967.

La Queste del Saint Graal. Ed. Albert Pauphilet. Paris: Champion, 1949.

The Quest of the Holy Grail. Trans. and introd. P. M. Matarasso. Baltimore: Penguin, 1969.

The Vulgate Cycle of Arthurian Romances. Ed. H. Oskar Sommer. 8 vols. Washington, D.C.: Carnegie, 1909–16.

Secondary Sources

Auerbach, Erich. *Mimesis: The Representation of Reality in Western Literature.* Trans. Willard Trask. Garden City, N.Y.: Doubleday, 1957.

Baumgartner, Emmanuèle. *L'Arbre et le pain: essai sur La Queste del Saint Graal.* Paris: SEDES, 1981.

Bennett, J. A. W., ed. *Essays on Malory.* Oxford: Clarendon Press, 1963.

Benson, Larry. *Malory's* Morte Darthur. Cambridge, Mass.: Harvard University Press, 1976.

Bloomfield, Morton. "Episodic Motivation and Marvels in Epic and Romance." In *Essays and Explorations: Studies in Ideas, Language, and Literature.* Cambridge, Mass.: Harvard University Press, 1970, pp. 97–128.

Bogdanow, Fanni. *The Romance of the Grail: A Study of the Structure and Genesis of a Thirteenth-Century Arthurian Prose Romance.* Manchester: Manchester University Press; New York: Barnes and Noble, 1966.

Brewer, D. S. "the hoole book." In *Essays on Malory.* Ed. J. A. W. Bennett. Oxford: Clarendon Press, 1963, pp. 41–63.

Brewer, D. S., ed. *Malory: The Morte Darthur.* Evanston, Ill.: Northwestern University Press, 1974.

Bruyne, Edgar de. *Etudes d'esthétique médiévale.* 3 vols. Bruges: De Tempel, 1946.

Chenu, M.-D. *Nature, Man and Society in the Twelfth Century.* Trans. Jerome Taylor and Lester K. Little. Chicago: University of Chicago Press, 1968.

Curtius, Ernst Robert. *European Literature and the Latin Middle Ages.* Trans. Willard R. Trask. New York: Harper and Row, 1953.

Fein, Susanna Greer. "Thomas Malory and the Pictorial Interlace of *La Queste del Saint Graal.*" *University of Toronto Quarterly,* 46 (1977), 215–40.

Field, P. J. C. *Romance and Chronicle: A Study of Malory's Prose Style.* Bloomington: Indiana University Press, 1971.

Focillon, Henri. *The Life of Forms in Art.* Trans. Charles Beecher Hogan and George Kubler. New York: Wittenborn, 1948.

Frankl, Paul. *Gothic Architecture*. In *The Pelican History of Art*. Ed. Nikolaus Pevsner. Trans. Dieter Pevsner. Baltimore: Penguin, 1962.

Frankl, Paul. *The Gothic: Literary Sources and Interpretations through Eight Centuries*. Princeton, N.J.: Princeton University Press, 1960.

Frankl, Paul. *Principles of Architectural History: The Four Phases of Architectural Style, 1420–1900*. Trans. and ed. James F. O'Gorman. Cambridge, Mass.: The MIT Press, 1968.

Frappier, Jean. *Etude sur La Mort Le Roi Artu*. 2nd ed. rev. and augmented. Geneva: Droz, 1968.

Frappier, Jean. "Le Graal et la chevalerie." *Romania*, 75 (1954), 165–210.

Frappier, Jean. "The Vulgate Cycle." In *Arthurian Literature in the Middle Ages*. Ed. Roger Sherman Loomis. Oxford: Clarendon Press, 1959, pp. 295–318.

Fries, Maureen. "The Tragic Pattern in Malory's *Morte Darthur*: Medieval Narrative as Literary Myth." In *The Early Renaissance* (Acta 5). Ed. Aldo S. Bernardo. Binghampton: State University of New York, 1979, pp. 81–99.

Gallo, Ernest. "Matthew of Vendôme: Introductory Treatise on the Art of Poetry." *Proceedings of the American Philosophical Society*, 118 (1974), 51–92.

Gallo, Ernest. "The *Poetria Nova* of Geoffrey of Vinsauf." In *Medieval Eloquence: Studies in the Theory and Practice of Medieval Rhetoric*. Ed. James J. Murphy. Berkeley and Los Angeles: University of California Press, 1978, pp. 68–84.

Gallo, Ernest. *The* Poetria Nova *and its Sources in Early Rhetorical Doctrine*. The Hague: Mouton, 1971.

Hauser, Arnold. *The Social History of Art*. Trans. Stanley Godman. New York: Vintage Books, 1959. Vol I.

Hennessy, Helen. "The Uniting of Romance and Allegory in *La Queste del Saint Graal*." *Boston University Studies in English*, 4 (1960), 189–201.

Hynes-Berry, Mary. "Malory's Translation of Meaning." *Studies in Philology*, 74 (1977), 243–57.

Ihle, Sandra Ness. "The Style of Partiality: Gothic Architecture and the Vulgate Cycle of Arthurian Romances." *Genre*, 6 (1973), 376–87.

Jordan, Robert. *Chaucer and the Shape of Creation*. Cambridge, Mass.: Harvard University Press, 1967.

Jung, Marc-René. *Etudes sur le poème allégorique en France au moyen age*. Romanica Helvetica, 82. Berne: Francke, 1971.

Kelly, Douglas. "*Matière* and *genera dicendi* in Medieval Romance." *Yale French Studies*, 51 (1974), 147–59.

Kelly, Douglas. "The Scope and Treatment of Composition in the Twelfth and Thirteenth-Century Arts of Poetry." *Speculum*, 41 (1966), 261–78.

Kelly, Douglas. "The Source and Meaning of *conjointure* in Chrétien's *Erec* 14." *Viator*, 1 (1970), 179–200.

Kelly, Douglas. "Theory of Composition in Medieval Narrative Poetry and Geoffrey of Vinsauf's *Poetria Nova*." *Mediaeval Studies*, 31 (1969), 119–30.

Kelly, Douglas. "Topical Invention in Medieval French Literature." In *Medieval Eloquence: Studies in the Theory and Practice of Medieval Rhetoric*. Ed. James J. Murphy. Berkeley and Los Angeles: University of California Press, 1978, pp. 231–51.

Kelly, Douglas. "*Translatio Studii*: Translation, Adaptation, and Allegory in Medieval French Literature." *Philological Quarterly*, 57 (1978), 287–310.

Kennedy, Edward D. "Malory and his English Sources." In *Aspects of Malory*. Ed. Toshiyuki Takamiya and Derek Brewer. Cambridge: D. S. Brewer; Woodbridge, Suffolk: Boydell and Brewer; Totowa, N.J.: Rowman and Littlefield, 1981.

Knight, Stephen T. "Some Aspects of Structure in Medieval Literature." *Parergon*, 16 (1976), 3–17.

Knight, Stephen T. *The Structure of Sir Thomas Malory's Arthuriad*. Australian Humanities Research Council Monograph 14. Sydney: Sydney University Press, 1969.

Köhler, Erich. *L'aventure chevaleresque: Idéal et réalité dans le roman courtois*. Trans. Eliane Kaufholz. Paris: Gallimard, 1974.

Kopp, Jane Baltzell. "Rhetorical 'Amplification' and 'Abbreviation' and the Structure of Medieval Narrative." *Pacific Coast Philology*, 2 (April, 1967), 32–39.

Lacy, Norris J. "Spatial Form in the *Mort Artu*." *Symposium*, 31 (1977), 337–45.

Lagorio, Valerie. "The Glastonbury Legends and the English Arthurian Grail Romances." *Neuphilologische Mitteilungen*, 79 (1978), 359–66.

Lambert, Mark. *Malory: Style and Vision in* Le Morte Darthur. New Haven: Yale University Press, 1975.

Leyerle, John. "The Interlace Structure of *Beowulf*." *University of Toronto Quarterly*, 37 (1967), 1–17.

Locke, Frederick William. "A New Approach to the Study of the *Queste del Saint Graal*." *Romanic Review*, 45 (1954), 241–50.

Locke, Frederick William. *The Quest for the Holy Grail: A Literary Study of a Thirteenth-Century French Romance*. Stanford, Calif.: Stanford University Press, 1960.

Lot, Ferdinand. *Etude sur le Lancelot en prose*. Paris: Champion, 1918.

Lubac, Henri de. *Exégèse médiévale: les quartre sens de l'Écriture*. 2 vols. Paris: Aubier, 1959–64.

Lumiansky, R. M. *Malory's Originality: A Critical Study of* Le Morte Darthur. Baltimore: Johns Hopkins University Press, 1964.

Matarasso, Pauline. *The Redemption of Chivalry: A Study of the* Queste del Saint Graal. Geneva: Droz, 1979.

Micha, Alexandre. "Etudes sur le Lancelot en prose: l'esprit du Lancelot-Graal." *Romania*, 82 (1961), 357–78.

Moorman, Charles. *The Book of Kyng Arthur: The Unity of Malory's* Morte Darthur. Lexington: University of Kentucky Press, 1965.

Moorman, Charles. "*The Tale of the Sankgreall*: Human Frailty." In *Malory's Originality*. Ed. R. M. Lumiansky. Baltimore: Johns Hopkins University Press, 1964, pp. 184–204.

Morse, Charlotte C. *The Pattern of Judgment in the* Queste *and* Cleanness. Columbia: University of Missouri Press, 1978.

Murphy, James J., ed. *Medieval Eloquence: Studies in the Theory and Practice of Medieval Rhetoric*. Berkeley and Los Angeles: University of California Press, 1978.

Muscatine, Charles. *Chaucer and the French Tradition*. Berkeley and Los Angeles: University of California Press, 1966.

Panofsky, Erwin, ed. *Abbot Suger on the Abbey Church of St.-Denis and its Art Treasures*. Princeton, N.J.: Princeton University Press, 1946.

Pauphilet, Albert. *Etudes sur la Queste del Saint Graal attribuée à Gautier Map*. Paris: Champion, 1968.

Quadlbauer, Franz. "Lukan im Schema des *ordo naturalis/artificialis*: ein Beitrag zur Geschichte der Lukanbewertung im lateinischen Mittelalter." *Grazer Beiträge*, 6 (1977), 67–105.

Robertson, D. W., Jr. *A Preface to Chaucer: Studies in Medieval Perspectives*. Princeton, N.J.: Princeton University Press, 1962.

Ryding, William. *Structure in Medieval Narrative*. The Hague: Mouton, 1971.

Savage, Grace Armstrong. "Father and Son in the *Queste del Saint Graal*." *Romance Philology*, 31 (1977), 1–16.

Savage, Grace Armstrong. "Narrative Technique in the *Queste del Saint Graal*." Ph.D. dissertation. Princeton, 1973.

Simes, G. R. "Chivalry and Malory's Quest of the Holy Grail." *Parergon*, 17 (1977), 37–42.

Simson, Otto von. *The Gothic Cathedral: Origins of Gothic Architecture and the Medieval Concept of Order*. 2nd ed. New York: Harper and Row, 1962.

Todorov, Tzvetan. *Poétique de la prose*. Paris: Seuil, 1971.

Tucker, P. E. "Chivalry in the *Morte*." In *Essays on Malory*. Ed. J. A. W. Bennett. Oxford: Clarendon Press, 1963, pp. 64–103.

Tuve, Rosemond. *Allegorical Imagery: Some Mediaeval Books and Their Posterity*. Princeton, N.J.: Princeton University Press, 1966.

Vinaver, Eugène. *Form and Meaning in Medieval Romance*. Cambridge: Modern Humanities Research Association, 1966.

Vinaver, Eugène. "Landmarks in Arthurian Romance." In *The Expansion and Transformation of Courtly Literature*. Ed. Nathanial B. Smith and Joseph T. Snow. Athens: The University of Georgia Press, 1980, pp. 17–31.

Vinaver, Eugène. *A la recherche d'une poétique médiévale*. Paris: Nizet, 1970.

Vinaver, Eugène. *The Rise of Romance*. Oxford: Clarendon Press, 1971.

Wellek, René, and Austin Warren. *Theory of Literature*. 3rd ed., rev. New York: A Harvest Book, 1956.

Wetherbee, Winthrop. *Platonism and Poetry in the Twelfth Century*. Princeton: N.J.: Princeton University Press, 1972.

Whitworth, Charles W. "The Sacred and the Secular in Malory's *Tale of the Sankgreal*." *Yearbook of English Studies*, 5 (1975), 19–29.

Worringer, Wilhelm. *Form in Gothic*. Trans. Sir Herbert Read. Rev. ed. New York: Schocken Books, 1957.

Zumthor, Paul. *Essai de poétique médiévale*. Paris: Seuil, 1972.

Index

JACKET DESIGNED BY MIKE JAYNES
COMPOSED BY PIED TYPER, LINCOLN, NEBRASKA
MANUFACTURED BY CUSHING-MALLOY, INC.,
ANN ARBOR, MICHIGAN
TEXT AND DISPLAY LINES IN PALATINO

Library of Congress Cataloging in Publication Data
Ihle, Sandra Ness, 1943–
Malory's Grail Quest.
Bibliography: pp. 189–94.
Includes index.
1. Malory, Thomas, Sir, 15th cent. Morte d'Arthur—
Sources. 2. Malory, Thomas, Sir, 15th cent. Morte
d'Arthur. 3. Queste del Saint Graal. 4. Grail—
Romances—History and criticism. I. Title.
PR2046.I36   1982   823'.2   82–70554
ISBN 0–299–09240–2